Miss Thang!
DESTINY FULFILLED

To: my queen
Danielle
my BFF
Love You Soooo
Love
Much!
xoxo

ANGELA WILSON

PRESENTS...

Miss Thang!

DESTINY FULFILLED

A Testimonial Guide to Divine Purpose and Greatness!

iUniverse, Inc.
New York   Bloomington

Miss Thang! Destiny Fulfilled
A Testimonial Guide to Divine Purpose and Greatness!

iUniverse books may be ordered through booksellers or by contacting:

iUniverse
1663 Liberty Drive
Bloomington, IN 47403
www.iuniverse.com
1-800-Authors (1-800-288-4677)

Because of the dynamic nature of the Internet, any Web addresses or links contained in this book may have changed since publication and may no longer be valid. The views expressed in this work are solely those of the author and do not necessarily reflect the views of the publisher, and the publisher hereby disclaims any responsibility for them.

ISBN: 978-1-4502-5537-0 (sc)
ISBN: 978-1-4502-5538-7 (ebk)

Printed in the United States of America

iUniverse rev. date: 08/27/2010

To my mom and dad, my biggest supporters

To London, my biggest fan

To my family, my biggest blessing

To God, my everything

Acknowledgments

F irst and foremost my Lord and Savior Jesus Christ. If I had ten thousand tongues to tell you how much I thank you, it would still not suffice. Jesus, my soul thirsts for you. My heart longs for you and my spirit is deep in love with you. Nothing I do can demonstrate my love, appreciation and thankfulness for being who you are to me--everything. This book is designed for your glory! Thank you Lord for first choosing me; a wretch undone and making me into the woman I am today. Your faithfulness, loving kindness and unconditional love is paying off! I readily stand before your throne to be an asset to the kingdom of God, spreading joy and inspiration through my personal journey. Thank you for trusting me. Thank you for this opportunity. Thank you for never giving up on me. Thank you Jesus for being my knight in shining armor. Let your glory be illuminated on each and every page.

To my son, London Mehki, my King in the making, the apple of my eye, thank you for teaching me how to be the best mom I can be. I am overjoyed because of your smile, innocent laugh, genius mentality, goofy personality and stunning good looks! I love you more than life itself. I am honored to be your mother. It's you and I against the world!

To my parents, Marvin and Patricia, the coolest and flyest parents on the planet! It would be terribly impossible to ask for a better set of parents. Parents who not only provided, but taught, guided, protected, and spoiled me into a strong, fearless go-getter! Nothing you do goes unnoticed. Everything you have done is appreciated. I love you too much for words to express. I hope I make you just as proud of me as I am of you.

To all naysayers, thank you for everything because if it were not for you, I wouldn't be so blessed as I am today. I appreciate the love and the hate. It is because of you I am blessed beyond measure. It is because of you I have a testimony to share. Thank you for giving me this testimony. The fire only perfected me. The best feeling in the world is doing what you said I can't! Success is the ultimate revenge.

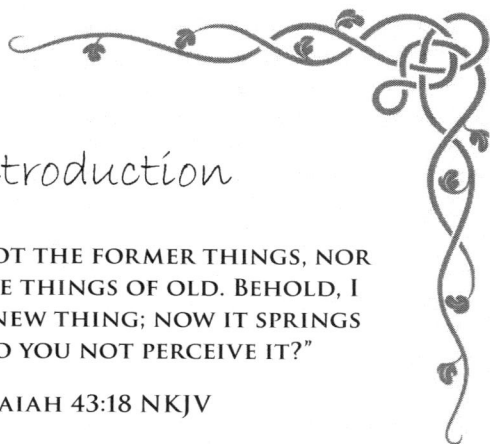

Introduction

"REMEMBER NOT THE FORMER THINGS, NOR
CONSIDER THE THINGS OF OLD. BEHOLD, I
AM DOING A NEW THING; NOW IT SPRINGS
FORTH, DO YOU NOT PERCEIVE IT?"

ISAIAH 43:18 NKJV

Girlfriends, God is busy! Oh yes, Honey, God is miraculously working in your life! Even if you can't see His manifestation; even if you can not feel Him, He's working! You picking up this book, right now, at this time in your life, at this very moment, is all for a reason! I believe its my divine purpose to share my testimony with you! Honey, I have experienced it all from an unfaithful fiance', child out of wedlock, fighting mistresses, I can go on and on! Allow me to take you on a journey, shall we? Starting from the beginning of my college career; freshman year at Ohio State University, to my spiritual and emotional downfall, to the birth of an unyoked, ungodly relationship, resulting in me scrambling for pieces of my broken heart, to salvation! Sleepless nights, depression and low self esteem all plagued me. Although I grew up in a Pentecostal church, unfortunately that was where my relationship with God started and ended; Sunday morning to Sunday afternoon. I lacked a true, genuine and growing connection and relationship with Him, and it showed. I didn't have the life Jesus died for me to live!

God proved to me firsthand how He really makes all things new! MAC counter makeovers don't hold a candle to the makeover God performs! I can't thank God enough for my valleys and trouble! Sometimes good things fall apart so better things can fall together! Now, don't put the book down and run for the hills! There is a purpose for this afterall. God taught me the hard way that valleys are all apart of the process. How could He possibly bring me out standing on a mountain top? God delivers you from down in the valley, not from the rooftop. Remember that! He's attempting to wake you up! And I have complete confidence that as you read through the pages of HIS book, co-authored by me, His light will shine into your life so bright your hands won't be big enough to hold what you receive. It all, however, starts with relationship. If you do not have a relationship with Christ, now is the time! You've lived in misery long enough! Look around and you'll see what the world has done for you...nothing. Now is the time to stop doing it your way, and start doing it Gods way! How many times has He proven your ways don't work? Will you let Him show you?

Don't you know that God is always thinking about you? Yes, He's thinking about you all the time! He wants to fellowship with you. Even in the midst of disobedience, God is on your side. God revealed to me that through my time of weakness, it was Him who had my back through it all. When my heart was broken, my soul was heavy and burdened and my mind was scrambled. But God never left my side. He wanted to sing me a love song! How good is God?! And what a sweet, sweet song it is, if I say so myself! He wants to sing to you too, Girlfriend! God wants to take you on a joy ride. Are you ready? Get out of your comfort zone! Sometimes we have to be broken in order to be restored. It was at my most vulnerable moment, when all my friends disappeared, when no one understood or even cared did I realize He was all I needed to begin with. God rescued me from a painful relationship I was struggling so hard to hold on to. I refused to let go, until it finally let go of me. Not until afterwards was it made known to me that God had so much more for me; a life so much better that it could not even be compared to what had left me. He had to strip me of an idol in my life. The very thing that was holding me back from my divine destiny had to go!

I almost drowned in my tears of unbearable pain and loneliness. I lost all hope. But notice I said, *almost*, right? God doesn't take us through deep waters to drown us- but to cleanse us. He knew what I could handle and what I couldn't; He showed me He really does know what's best for me despite my foolish doubts and fluttering insecurities. As God picked me up, consumed by all my mess, His tender loving arms revealed my mistakes and illustrated how they needed to be corrected. He ushered me into a intimate relationship with Him, on a level that I had never been before! Daily, He shows me who He is, and how much He loves me, despite my flaws. He gently convicted me in the midst of my disobedience; my distance from Christ reflected in everything I did and did not do. I was miserable and unhappy. I was living without purpose; opting for temporary pleasures instead of lasting life. I was looking to a man to provide validation and love. I gave him power over me; a power no one but Jesus should have. Resting my expectations in a man instead of God led me to nothing but disaster! Shortly thereafter I found myself crying on my knees, crawling back to my first love, God.

He never ceases to amaze me. Gods Word promises, "…all things work for the good for those who love God and are called according to His purpose"(Romans 8:28). Even in the midst of a valley, the fire is a requirement to move forward. I now have a testimony unlike any other! I want to share my journey with you, Sista! We're in this together! God is still molding me and shaping me into the woman He destined for me to be all along, a Proverbs 31 woman! (But more on that later)!

Picking up this book and reading this far is the first step to divine purpose and greatness. Divided into two sections, this book is similar to that a story. But with this story you can skip from chapter to chapter; starting with the areas you believe are in need of the most improvement. The first section is entitled, *Basic.* I call it this because before we come to know Christ, basic is the best descriptive word that describes us! Living without abundance, peace, joy, favor and provision, we live life as the world does. We love what it loves, only to receive what it gives. How many times has the world let you down? Hurt your feelings, abandoned or betrayed you? Too many to count, right? Now count how many times God has failed you. Try to remember when a need went unfulfilled, when He didn't forgive you for repeated mistakes, when He lied on you, gave up on you, disrespected you or told you He didn't love you anymore? Is there any comparison? When we enter into a relationship with God, we become fly, because that is exactly what we do. We fly above our old selves, habits, and lifestyles and instantly we are advanced to higher ground. Still not convinced? Look around you and compare the lives of the children of God to that of a basic woman. Gods work speaks for itself!

Will you take this journey with me to greatness? God has a wonderful destiny for you Miss Thang, but can you handle it? Come take this heavenly voyage and spiritual and emotional cleansing trip that'll upgrade you from basic to fly! As you learn more about your heavenly Father, He will reveal Himself to you, crafting you to be the woman you were intended to be. Are you ready to be promoted?

Table of Contents

FROM BASIC...

To Fly!:

So, who is Miss Thang?

~Miss Thang! is one who is confident, yet humble, intelligent, yet teachable, stylish, yet polished, educated, yet studies daily. She electrifies the room with her presence, attracting all eyes to her inner glow and unforgettable smile. She is captivating, delicately crafted with a sincere heart, a tongue coated with love and an expectant helping hand. Her eyes glisten, her heart is passionate; her head on straight, flair just right. Three inch heels are considered her flats, she struts like the woman God fashioned her to be. She drips of divine favor; swag is addicted to her, confidence exudes her and destiny awaits her. Rebelling against trends, she marches to be the beat of her own drum. *Miss Thang!* does not fit in, for she was not designed to. She was perfectly crafted as an upgrade; a woman of stature and distinction. She knows favors unfair; facing lifes challenges head on, knowing in advance she already has the victory. She is well aware haters are closet fans. She follows Gods lead, surrendering to her Heavenly Father, as He orders her steps and lights her path. She. Is. Miss. Thang.

~Destiny: An event that will occur inevitably in the future; fate. Aware of her purpose on earth, *Miss Thang*! seeks her heavenly

1

Father to prepare her steps, guide her walk, hold her hand, and walk along side her. As she rides this journey called life, God is the driver and she is the trusting, loyal, dependent passenger; she permits God to be God. She wins at all costs, because as a child of God, even when she lose, she wins. All things work together for her benefit; the good, the bad, and the ugly. She does not question, instead, she trusts. *Miss Thang!* knows that without a relationship with God, her life would be chaotic; lack of order, provision, protection and harmony. Determination, hard work and goal setting acts as only a diminutive portion to achieving her destiny, and even those are not promise fulfillers because she knows God is the ultimate author and finisher of her faith, making her crooked roads straight and shielding her along the way.

~Fulfilled: A dream, promise, a desire brought into actuality; effectively executing a want, to put in effect, to carry out. *Miss Thang!* is fully aware that God does not make mistakes. She knows what God has for her, is for her, and nothing can be done about it. *Miss Thang!* acknowledges that God completes whatever He starts. He delicately placed predestined dreams on her heart, purpose over her very existence, and fulfills everything she has ever longed for. She is fulfilled with more blessings than she can hold, with unspeakable peace and coveted victory. She is fulfilled in every definition of the word.

~Greatness: Outstanding importance, authority. Greatness is the epitome of eminence, larger than life and gracefulness. *Miss Thang!* has much more than the ordinary- she is furthest from average. Mediocracy is allergic to her. Her joy, her peace, her sense of self is not related to material possessions, but from God and Him alone. In Him, her needs are met, her voids are filled, and all doubts

are silenced. Divinely, purposefully, and beautifully crafted, *Miss Thang!* is the apple of Gods eye. Greatness awaits her, as history books anticipate the very details she is destined to create.

Is this you?

From Basic...

Simple, Composed of Only the
Necessary Features, Regular,
Minimal, Absence of Luxury, Plain,
Undefined, the Most Common,
Average, General, Unsophisticated

A New Beginning

"AND HE WHO WAS SEATED ON THE THRONE
SAID, "BEHOLD, I AM MAKING ALL THINGS NEW."

REVELATION 21:5

Ecclesiastes 3:1 reads, "To everything there is a season, a time for every purpose under heaven." One of the most devastating mistakes a woman can make is failing to recognize the season she's in. When this occurs, doubt, frustration, and unhappiness all start a downward spiraling mental and emotional downfall. Circumstances and decisions become forced. You answer your own prayers, make excuses, justify and reason in defense of poor judgment. Your blossoming relationship with God becomes hindered; expecting God to come through the front door when He is daily preparing you from the backyard. Strengthening your character, developing a mature relationship with Him and bearing fruit are just a few ways God perfects you. You may be dealing with an angry and demeaning boss at work, but little do you know God is using your boss to instill qualities of patience, understanding and a spirit of love to those who dislike you. In the midst of a storm, you may have to endure a season of financial lack. God is teaching you the value of money; tithing ten percent of your income, budgeting, prioritizing and wise spending. That is

what I mean when I refer to the "front door" and the "back yard".
God uses what you think is a horrifying life ending experience
into your biggest triumph. You look to God to deliver you from
an unfulfilling job when He is preparing you to start your own
corporation!

It's first imperative to define what a spiritual season is. Spiritual
seasons are purely created for your greatest spiritual growth and
greatest season of fruit bearing and sowing. They are designed
to create and develop your character, bringing you to a place of
spiritual maturity. Seasons can also be determined by the people
in your life. One person can affect the start or end of a season.
The entrance, exit, or separation of a person in your life all affect
what season you transition into, or stay in.

As you start on your journey to internal inventory and
emotional cleansing, you must first take your share of the blame
for any unhappiness you may experience. Today, excuses will no
longer be made. Playing the blame game will only get you so far.
It's time to start taking responsibility for your circumstances and
unfulfillment. Yes, Sistas, we share a portion of the blame; no
one hurt you, used you, etc. that you did not allow. Misfortune
did not occur without you first setting it up. Your back can only
be rode if it's bent. It's time to start being protective over yourself
and handle yourself with care!

God provides everyone with free will; the right to make our
own choices and allowing us to make our own mistakes. But
despite our pitfalls and flaws, He's always there to pick us up, with
open arms. He patiently waits on our return to His unchanging
hand. He hates to see His children in pain and suffering from
the result of irresponsible and flawed decisions. But He never
judges us, He continues to look out for us and protect us even
in the midst of all our messiness. For me, I chose to stay in a

emotionally abusive relationship that became detrimental to my health, mind, self-esteem, and relationship with Christ, or lack thereof. I was fully aware of the type of person I was involved with the initial time his true self was revealed, but I chose to go back. I returned willingly and fully aware. And boy did I pay for it! For every action, there is a reaction; consequences to every decision. I finally took responsibility for my actions of selfishness and a love struck mentality.

We all play a role in what happens in our life. In our gut, what some would call a womans intuition, I call a divine conscious which allows us to sense whether a situation is upright and acceptable or wrong and unsuitable. It also guides us and tells us what we need to do for our own well being and security. Oh, how the Lord works in mysterious ways! Oh, how the Holy Spirit warns us and we refuse to listen! Have you ever made a decision and immediately after think, "I should have followed my first mind!?" Well guess what Sistas, that first mind was the voice of God. His Holy Spirit directs and conducts us, giving us a defining impression, or gut feeling that something is wrong. But when God reveals to us something we don't want to believe, we tend to retreat, backing away and refusing to accept what is staring us in the face. We ask for signs from God, "Oh, God give me a sign! Give me a sign!" But when He does, and we receive an answer we don't want, we convince ourselves that voice was just out to get us! We rationalize, make excuses, and justify. We fail to realize that God answers all of our prayers, sometimes He just says no. God allows us to endure tough challenges to make us stronger and to build our character and increase our faith in Him. It is impossible to have a storm testimony without the storm.

It is difficult to appreciate the sun when you have never experienced the downpour of rain. But rain is indeed necessary for growth. Think of the beautiful flowers of the earth. They grow by sunlight, but also by rain. In their destined season, they blossom into one of natures most gorgeous gifts! Believe it or not, God is working on YOU! Yes, you! He's perfecting you, molding you into the woman He wants you to be. What is so great about God is that He sees the best in you, when everyone else can see nothing but the worst. He sees your potential, despite where you are now. It's Gods desire to upgrade you! He knows exactly what He's doing, but you have to let Him do it! There is no need to play Holy Ghost Junior! He does not need your help, thank you very much! God has a perfect plan for you. You will understand it more, by and by. Remember, behind your biggest obstacle lies your biggest blessing! When you pass the test of faith and endurance, you will experience joy beyond all understanding! The plans God has for you are so extraordinary that He promises you, "No eye has seen, no ear has heard, no mind has imagined what God has in store for those who love him" (1 Corinthians 2:9). Learn to trust God with everything. He is all that you could ever need. God delights in making you happy. Although He has many children, He can make you feel like the only one! With God, you never have to worry if you can trust Him, or whether He will leave you.

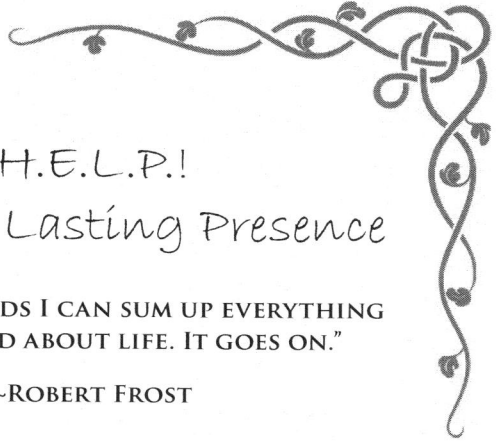

H.E.L.P.!
His Ever Lasting Presence

"IN THREE WORDS I CAN SUM UP EVERYTHING
I'VE LEARNED ABOUT LIFE. IT GOES ON."

~ROBERT FROST

Sometimes as we look to our past, we fail to focus on our present, therefore keeping us stagnant and unproductive. We look to the trials we've overcome- occasionally wishing what happened hadn't. Since time traveling is not an option, we tend to sabotage ourselves, mentally, emotionally and spiritually. We feel so hurt and so disappointed that if the person who offended us has not apologized, we wallow in pain. Our past is similar to that of a movie screen; a reflection of our yesterdays, playing over and over again to remind us of where we've been, and what we've successfully endured. I can not retrieve those painful years of my life. I can not uncry my tears or undo any pain or misfortune. Although I can not undo it, the payoff was well worth it! I received a new found relationship with Jesus Christ, which is priceless.

In a televised sermon I witnessed awhile back, the pastor preached on the art of letting go and completely casting our pain on God. She instructed Gods people to not look to the person who hurt us or offended us for restoration, because they will never be capable of healing and restoring us. Only God can give you back everything you lost. Only Jesus can restore your soul. Only Jesus can heal your broken heart, burdened soul, and festering feelings of sadness. You must look to God; to not only start with Him but also finish with Him. If anything, you should look to your transgressors and thank them. Thank them for their actions, because if it was not for them, you would still be in the same place you were before, never progressing and never upgrading. Our God is a God of more than enough! He does not intend for you to just make it, but to have an abundance of everything. And because of their actions, Gods attention was caught and He immediately sought to your rescue! Send your offenders a thank you card!

The Bible says, " For I know the plans I have for you," declares the LORD, "plans to prosper you and not to harm you, plans to give you hope and a future " (Jeremiah 29:11 NIV). God has a plan and a strong desire for you beyond your wildest dreams! If you want to make God laugh, tell Him your plans! Tell Him what you want to do, and when your plans are compared to His, you will surely see who really knows what's best! God has so much for you, but He can not give it to you if your harboring feelings of hate, unforgiveness and resentment. These feelings are not of God. So, God will not bestow His divine blessing, because the feelings of joy and restoration can not coincide with hate.

I struggled with letting go and completely releasing the strong hurtful feelings that I was harboring for years! Until I realized that the man who hurt me did not care, never mind healing me. Isn't it ironic how we tend to walk around with anger in our hearts, while the person who hurt us is walking around without a care in the world? It wasn't until then that I realized he was not capable to give me back what he took from me. My joy, my smile, my peace of mind. It was out of his power to be so giving. I gave a man power over me, basing my feelings strictly off of what he did and did not do. His actions affected me in every way because I was foolishly dependent on him. I had to have an A.S.A.P. attitude, always saying a prayer, looking first to God to help me.

So I took every piece of my heart, placed them in the hands of God, and continued to P.U.S.H., praying until something happened. That was my only option because everyone else who I trusted failed me. God knew exactly what to do with me, and Jesus more than made up for it! Praise God! God restored me double what I lost, or what I thought I lost. God gave more to me than I could ever imagine! I lost my joy, but now I have joy abundantly. I lost my peace, but now I have peace that surpasses all understanding! My latter days will be greater than my former. What I thought I lost, what I thought was stripped from me, what I thought I could not live without, ushered me into my perfect, awaiting destiny. Everyday I say, "Thank you, God!"- I made it! I survived whatever life threw my way, and so can you! Sistas, it's time to start celebrating some peoples exit from your life! They may be hindering you from where God wants you to be. God wants to elevate you, but stragglers and tag alongs are not allowed to accompany you. It is time to start celebrating those closed doors and opportunities you may feel you missed. They are all for your benefit.

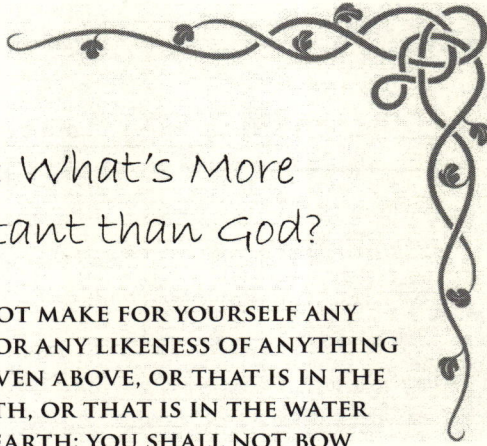

Idols: What's More Important than God?

YOU SHALL NOT MAKE FOR YOURSELF ANY
CARVED IMAGE, OR ANY LIKENESS OF ANYTHING
THAT IS IN HEAVEN ABOVE, OR THAT IS IN THE
EARTH BENEATH, OR THAT IS IN THE WATER
UNDER THE EARTH; YOU SHALL NOT BOW
DOWN TO THEM NOR SERVE THEM. FOR I, THE
LORD YOUR GOD, AM A JEALOUS GOD...

SECOND COMMANDMENT

Anything that you place a higher value on or prioritize before God is considered an idol; something you greatly admire, feel is owed to you, a desire or value. An idol can be anything from money, to cars, to men, even to your career. If you put more focus on it than you do your relationship with God, it's inevitable that it becomes more important to you. It holds more significance to you and ultimately rules over you. An idol can also be reflected in how you spend your time. Throughout your work day, do you talk to God? Do you tell Him how you're doing? Do you praise Him and ask for His guidance? Or do you pray only when you need something? After work, how do you spend your time? Think about the time you spend at work, school, shopping, and any other extra curricular activity. Now compare that to the time you spend with Jesus. Compare that time to how much of yourself you give to your church and community. What you give your time to, is what's most important to you. How you spend your time reveals character. Because you will always make time for what you really want to do. If your mind is set on buying new Christian Louboutin pumps the very next paycheck, you will make a way out of no way and buy those new Christian Louboutin pumps the very next paycheck. And nothing can keep you from it! Oh, the power of the mind! We always make a way for what we want, don't we?

Nothing can stop you from what you have your mind set on. So what are you giving your mind to? What in your life is an idol because you give it more time, energy, and attention than you do Jesus? Is God left with fleeting prayers between meetings and outings with girlfriends, or do you spend quality time talking to Him? Prayer is an ongoing conversation with God, emphasis on the word *ongoing*, which can be done anywhere and anytime. Prayer is talking with God. You do not have to be by the side of your bed on your knees, fingers crossed, eyes closed, face washed, hair pulled back with a white prayer shawl over your back with sandals next to a bottle of blessed oil! Prayer is constant interaction with Christ. Remember, He is your friend and He is anxious to hear from you! It is when you allow other things in your life to take precedence over your relationship with Him is when idols are created.

God is a jealous God! The first commandment states that you should not have any other gods before Him. My previous relationship was my idol. Do you give a man more time and attention than you give Christ? Instead of praying and reading your Word, do you take care of your job assignments before you acknowledge Gods presence? God desperately wants you to realize who first loved you! Don't search for fulfillment in other places, because rest assured you will come up short every single time you try. Anything you feel you have to have can be used as an instrument against you. Your enemy can use what you think you need for your spiritual demise. When you realize that God is all you have, you realize God is all you need. God understood me, was patient with me, and loved me like none other. He is now first in my life. He now has my undivided attention. I'd rather submit now than be broken down later. I'd much rather surrender now than be stripped later.

The first thing I do when I awake in the morning is say a prayer before my feet touches the carpet. I whisper a soft, "Thank you Jesus," for his brand new mercy every morning. I thank Him for protecting my family and I while asleep, and allowing me to witness one more day. It is Gods angels who watch over us at night, keeping us safe from all harm seen and unseen. He keeps a hedge around us, keeping us close to Him at all times. Thank him when you wake up. Make it the first thing you do. Did you wake up in your right mind? Do you have a roof over your head, food to eat and clothes to wear? If so, you owe God praise! It does not have to be as good as it is. Thank Him for His grace, for we are all sinners and we are all undeserving. We all fall short of the glory. I thank Jesus for dying for me. It is because of Him that little old me, a wretch undone, has been redeemed from the blood Christ shed, just for you and me.

Do some spiritual cleansing and evaluate what exactly in your life is taking away from your relationship with God. What has become so important to you that what God has is now second best? Start every morning off with Christ. While getting prepared for my day, I play my encouraging, gospel music. When I leave the house, the joy I feel is so overwhelming I feel like I'm floating! I can feel his presence all around me and His light shines bright through me throughout the entire day! I guess that is why everyone stares...

MISS THANGS LIFE QUOTE:

"I think everybody should get rich and famous and do everything they ever dreamed of so they can see that it's not the answer."

~Jim Carey

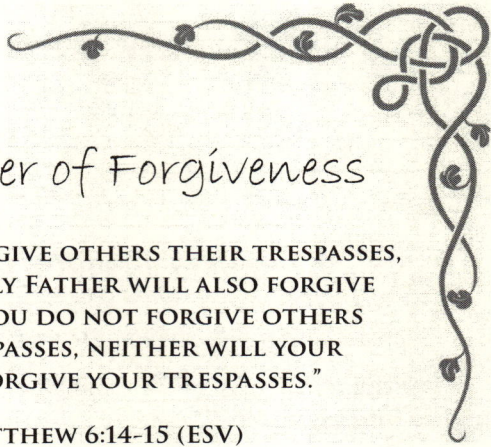

The Power of Forgiveness

"FOR IF YOU FORGIVE OTHERS THEIR TRESPASSES,
YOUR HEAVENLY FATHER WILL ALSO FORGIVE
YOU, BUT IF YOU DO NOT FORGIVE OTHERS
THEIR TRESPASSES, NEITHER WILL YOUR
FATHER FORGIVE YOUR TRESPASSES."

MATTHEW 6:14-15 (ESV)

F orgiveness is defined as a pardon for an offense, ceasing restitution or punishment. Forgiveness is so important to God, but its concept can be a hard pill to swallow. Releasing all claim of an offense, debt or wrong doing can feel like a daunting task. My past relationship taught me firsthand the notion of what it really meant to truly forgive someone. After it was revealed to me that my fiance` impregnated another woman who I shared backyards with, my world fell apart! And in that destroyed world, I attempted to make the relationship work again, even after I was lied to, embarrassed and devastated because everyone knew about it except me. Failed attempts to make it work made my life an emotional rollercoaster. Even though I was naively willing to try again, unforgiveness, anger and bitterness hindered me from any healing and restoration. How could I forgive him when I could not trust him? Needless to say, our irretrievable and blemished relationship came to a permanent end.

18

We continued in circles for nearly a year; coupling up to deciding on being friends to enemies and back around again. It was a vicious cycle. I harbored tremendous pain. It took years to let go. My, how far I have come! And it's all because of Jesus. I think about how God brought me through, grabbing my hand and never letting go. I easily could have lost my mind or my life. One split second decision in anger could have changed my whole life! Due to the emotional turmoil I experienced, you would think I would be in a mental institution! But by the grace of God, I don't look like what I been through. When you don't look like the hell you've been through, you know you have favor!

Through it all He protected, shielded, and upgraded me. Jesus treated me better than I treated myself! He undoubtedly remained faithful to me, more than I could have ever been to myself. God sees the big picture, for He is the "...author and finisher of our faith"(Hebrew 12:2 NKJV), while we only see what He allows us to. God communicates with us on a strict need to know basis. He wants us to trust Him every step of the way.When I failed to think about what was best for me, Jesus stepped in and gave me hope! The burden became too heavy to carry, but I knew I had no choice but to forgive. The only way I could have moved forward was by letting go of the past. God will work on the person who hurt you, only after you get over it. After *you* let it go, you then release God to do what only He can do to the offender.

When I thought about forgiving someone, I considered it as a sick way of letting them off the hook. I believed by forgiving them, their behavior would be viewed as acceptable and without proper consequence. I felt that if you forgave someone, you weren't supposed to be angry with them. And to me, being angry with a person would make them feel bad. They would eventually see how mad I am and it would make them feel remorseful. This philosophy, of course, was incorrect and needless to say it did not work. When I failed to forgive, all I did was keep myself bound in pain. When I didn't exonerate, it was I, who harbored feelings that affected all my actions. It took more of my energy to be sad. (Consequently, did you know that it requires more bones in your face to form a frown then to smile?) The body was structured to be happy!

Being mad is emotionally, mentally, physically, and most importantly, spiritually draining! Most health concerns are directly related to stress. That's why doctors ask about your level of stress because it is directly related to your body's wellbeing. Your body was designed to harbor joy! God designed you that way to enjoy life and to live it more abundantly! We were not designed to hold grudges and bare unforgiveness, because Jesus does not hold grudges against us. Jesus forgives us every time we sin against Him. He does not remember them, complain about them or bring them up to remind us of our mistakes. The story of the unmerciful servant in Matthew 18: 21-23 explains how Jesus feels about forgiveness,

"Then Peter came to Jesus and asked, "Lord, how many times shall I forgive my brother when he sins against me? Up to seven times? Jesus answered, "I tell you, not seven times, but seventy times seven. Therefore, the kingdom of heaven is like a king who wanted to settle accounts with his servants."

In Matthew 6: 15 (NIV), Jesus explains, "If you do not forgive men their sins, your Father will not forgive your sins." It is our responsibility to forgive, just as Jesus forgives us. How many times do you disappoint Him? How many times a day do you ponder unclean thoughts, act on malicious motives, or speak with an ungodly tongue? And how many times does God forgive you?

Jesus does not ask His people to do something He does not give us sufficient grace and strength to carry out. He would not ask us "to love your neighbor as yourself" (Mark 12:33), without first providing His grace and divine help to do so. This is the same as forgiveness. Forgiveness is for your benefit and peace of mind. I know it's easier said than done, but I encourage you that there is hope. Forgiveness has nothing to do with your offender at all, but everything to do with you! God revealed to me that harboring dangerous animosity and hateful feelings towards my ex, did nothing more than hinder my relationship with Him. My ex had moved on and could have cared less about my anger. I was the one who was stuck in my own pity party. I was having a grand of a time feeling sorry for myself, while my ex couldn't have been happier.

Unforgiveness is related to resentment. Resentment is like drinking poison and waiting for the other person to die, which does not make any sense. Forgiving releases pain. When you don't forgive, your offender maintains power over you. They live in your mind rent free! For instance, if every time you see them you get angry, you have given them power. Thus having dominion over your emotions. No one should have that kind of authority over you. Remember, you should never let someone pull you so low that you hate them. It is never worth it. No one should be worth your energy or precious time to hate them. You have better things to do, and greater and better goals to accomplish!

One trick to forgiveness is to write a letter. Write everything that you're feeling on paper and let it flow. Once completed, burn it. While burning the letter in a safe place, verbally express that you release them, and any pain and disappointment you may have felt burns along with the paper. Anytime the offense comes to mind, simply say "transfer." This is a way of releasing your pain to God, the God of all wonders who understands exactly what you're going through. When no one else cares, God does. When you feel alone, Jesus knows just what to do. Remember, Jesus was betrayed and setup by one of His twelve disciples, Judas. Peter, another disciple, professed his loyalty, claiming he would not betray Jesus. But he denied Jesus not once, not twice, but three times! God knows what it is like to be disappointed and hurt. He knows what you are going through, and a simple "transfer" will help place your burden at the holy feet of Christ whenever the thought becomes too painful to bare.

Once you forgive your offender, your work is far from over. You now must forgive yourself. Forgive yourself for not heeding unto Gods instruction. Forgive yourself for not taking care of yourself, searching for fulfillment in everything and everyone but God, the one who fulfills your every need and desire. Forgive yourself for disobeying Gods commandments. He knows your ways and He provides instruction on how to conduct yourself in His Word. His directions and commands are for your protection! He loves you unconditionally. He is your first love. Trust Christ as your only Savior because, "He first loved you" (1 John 4:19). God loves you just the way you are. He does not make any mistakes, for He created you in His image.

Jesus proved His agape love by dying on Calvary for you. It hurts God to see you distressed and in pain. Just as a mother hurts when her child is anguished; God hurts to see you cry. But God allows you to make your mistakes and make your own decisions. It's called free will. Nevertheless, God never fails to be there for you at all times. Forgive yourself for not heeding to red flags and ignoring God's warning signs. When you forgive yourself, you become free! You can forgive those around you and you can take responsibility for yourself.

MISS THANGS LIFE QUOTE:

"If you put a small value on yourself, you can be sure the world won't raise your price. So handle yourself with care."

Repentance: The Key to Spiritual Growth

"BUT UNLESS YOU REPENT, YOU TOO WILL PERISH."

LUKE 13:3 NIV

Praise be to God that He is not like us! We are so fortunate to have a God of limitless forgiveness, infinite mercy and unfathomable grace. Even though we are daughters of the King, covered in anointing and favored among women, we commit offenses and sin on a daily basis. We need Gods divine help every second of the day. We need His gentle conviction and genuine all loving assistance to do better next time; successfully learning our lesson and passing future tests. A day does not pass by when transgressions are not committed in the eyes of God. This includes our actions, words, and thoughts. Which is why it is so crucial to guard your mind; to think about what you're thinking about.

Everything that you act on, starts first with a thought. Lingering, negative thoughts lead to negative words, therefore leading into negative, and irreversible actions. Philippians 4:8-9 (NLT) describes what we should give our minds to: "Fix your thoughts on what is true, and honorable, and right, and pure, and lovely, and admirable. Think about things that are excellent and worthy of praise. Keep putting into practice all you learned and received from me--everything you heard from me and saw me doing. Then the God of peace will be with you." God knows the importance of your thoughts, for what you give your mind to is shown through your actions and words.

Sin separates you from God by severing your bond and placing a strangling grip on your relationship with Him. When you sin, your spirit becomes tainted, and because your Savior is without sin, it is impossible for dark and light to walk together. When I get a dose of God, a closer encounter with Him, I yearn for more! Boy, is He addictive! The more I get, the more I want. Everyday I am desperate to know Him better by drawing in closer to Him and feeling a deeper presence. When we are disobedient to God's Word, going left when He instructs us to go right, our relationship is hindered and wounded; until we approach Him humbly and genuinely asking for forgiveness. With a sincere heart, God will indeed hear your call and grant forgiveness. In Psalm 103:12 (NLT), God "...removes our sins as far from us as the east is from the west." Isaiah 43:25 reads, "I, even I, am the one who wipes out your transgressions for My own sake, and I will not remember your sins." God knows everything about us, including our faults, weaknesses, and strengths. He knows we are weak and in need of Him and his divine forgiveness, which He never fails provide time and time again. When we come to Him for forgiveness, we repent and confess our wrongdoing. Repentance is the sincere remorse of past conduct; self-reproach for what one has done or failed to do. It's ceasing against all sin and turning to God with an admittance of guilt. Repentance is "looking at it Gods way." That is one of the many key elements to spiritual growth; always moving forward and closer to God.

Though God forgives our sins, the consequences of our actions continue to linger. Regardless of what we do, consequences always add up. The way in which we treat people, the decisions we make, our conduct and what we value all can operate to the glory of God, or work for evil. Galatians 6: 8 (NIV) describes how we reap what we sow: "The one who sows to please his sinful nature, from that nature will reap destruction; the one who sows to please the Spirit, from the Spirit will reap eternal life." God will allow us to reap what we sow to bring us to a place of true repentance. Sometimes we never truly realize the devastating effects of our actions until we experience it for ourselves. God allows what we have done to others to be done to us, to usher us into a deeper understanding of the consequences and cost of everything we do. We then recognize and understand our consequences. And depending on the severity of the case, it causes us to feel remorseful, bringing us to a position of pure repentance, regret and penitence. As you experience varying circumstances, ask yourself whether you are sowing or reaping. Are you sowing spiritual seeds, or reaping what you've done to another individual? The penalty of your actions will always find you, designed to help you learn from your mistakes.

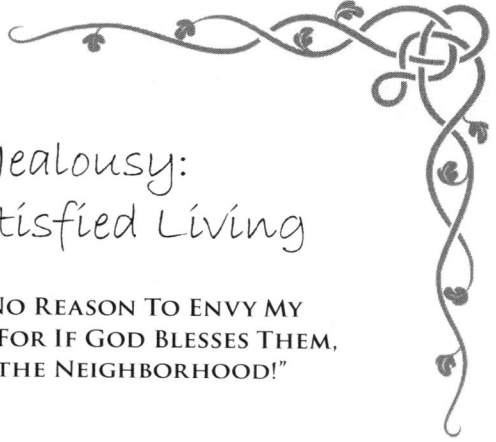

Jealousy:
Unsatisfied Living

"I HAVE NO REASON TO ENVY MY NEIGHBOR, FOR IF GOD BLESSES THEM, HE'S IN THE NEIGHBORHOOD!"

"A peaceful heart leads to a healthy body; jealousy is like cancer in the bones" (Proverbs 14:30 NLT). Jealousy is a bitter attitude and a destructive, downbeat way of thinking. It's a distressing and cheerless lifestyle filled with unhappiness because you long for what you don't have and covet what others have. The spirit of jealousy is a toxic one; a smack in God's face because you hold feelings of discontentment. You feel envious over His generosity. You may feel God has somehow made a mistake with you, looked you over, and forgot all about you! You may feel a sense of false entitlement, which is extremely dangerous because God is not obligated by any means. God has provided you with all the necessities of life. You may not possess everything you yearn for, but everything you need is provided. Is it not? I have never seen the righteous forsaken, have you? You can rest in the fact that God knows exactly what He's doing. Why would God bless you with something that will end up taking your focus off of Him?

God asks, "If you're not even satisfied with what I have given you, why should I give you something else to complain about?" Despite our pity parties and false sense of knowing what is best for us, God knows what is best. He teaches us accountability and responsibility. Are you responsible and mature enough to handle what you pray for? In certain situations, sometimes the grass looks greener on the other side. Please find peace and comfort in the fact that you do not know the journey of others. You will never know what is going on behind closed doors. And why should you? If you put even the slightest amount of energy, thought and time on God as you do being consumed in the business of anothers, you would be too ecstatic and blessed to even consider the blessings of others. A mature Christian woman does not covet because there is no room in her heart for it is so overjoyed with what she has. She is so focused on her relationship with God that she does not have the time to compare and contrast her life with others. Her heart is filled with thankfulness and her tongue is always rejoicing! When she thinks about how far God has brought her, all she can do is praise God! Because when the praises go up, blessings come down!

After my break up, I was lonesome and secluded myself. Although I had been alone, God illustrated the fact that I am never truly lonely. He is always present. He "...is close to the brokenhearted and saves those who are crushed in the spirit" (Psalm 34:18 NKJV). God will never leave you or forsake you! God loves you more than you can ever imagine, so much that He sent his only son to die for you. What friend do you have who is innocent of all wrongdoing, but would take the fall for you? What friend would lay down His life for you, so you can have a relationship with Him and His Father? While He was hanging on the cross, He was thinking about you! Every step Jesus took closer to death, He had you on His mind. I encourage you to be thankful for what you have, and thankful for what you don't. Take a minute and simply observe your family and everything around you. What if at this very minute, God took it all away? Do you appreciate how blessed you are?

God is preparing you for greatness! What God has for you, is for you, and there is nothing anyone can do about it! Everything you need, God never fails to provide. Trust Him. God sees your sincere heart, and He knows the desires of your heart. He's the one that gave you them! But only in His time will He bring forth the blessings of the earth. The test is in the time. The test is in how you operate when all you have is time! The ultimate assessment and true sign of a mature woman is in how she acts when she has what she wants, and how she acts when she does not have what she wants. Will she curse God? Is her praise purely conditional; based solely on whether her bills are paid or if she receives a blessing? Is she an unconditional worshipper? Is she like Job of the Bible? Could God look down upon her and brag about her? Would He want to show her off, because He can count on her in pleasant and adverse times to give Him praise? He blesses those who are not only readers of His Word, but those who are also doers of His Word. It is when you concentrate on this, that envy will not even be capable of existing in a heart filled with the Holy Spirit.

MISS THANGS LIFE QUOTE:

"God, if I can't have what I want, let me want what I have."
~Author Unknown

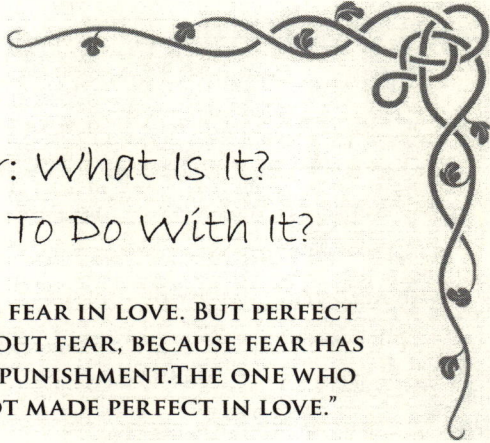

Fear: What Is It?
What To Do With It?

"THERE IS NO FEAR IN LOVE. BUT PERFECT
LOVE DRIVES OUT FEAR, BECAUSE FEAR HAS
TO DO WITH PUNISHMENT. THE ONE WHO
FEARS IS NOT MADE PERFECT IN LOVE."

1 JOHN 4:18 NIV

Change can be a very challenging matter to endure. Dependent on the situation, it can be a fearful transition, but a mature woman, however, accepts change. A full-grown and settled woman welcomes God to work in her life, even if that means stripping toxic people and things from her life. Fear usually accompanies change. Change represents the unknown, and we experience apprehension when we feel we are not in control. That's the beauty of God, He is in control and because of Jesus, we can rest in His arms, not having to worry about anything. Gods Word explains in 2 Timothy 1:7 (NKJV), "That God hath not given us the spirit of fear, but of power, and of love, and a sound mind." Fear is what we feel when we are led to do something we do not want to do. Fear is the result of faithlessness. When we do not depend on God, we dabble in disobedience and exercise excuses and panic. We ask God to work in our lives, and the minute something changes we scream to the high heavens, "What are you doing?!" Fear and confusion are the best of friends, walking hand and hand to halt your spiritual progress and growth. An appropriate amount of fear, however, can actually be healthy. When we encounter anxiety, that's when we fight our hardest. We relentlessly give our all; tears, sweat and blood when we are aware that something valuable is on the line. We tend not to fight as hard when we are in our comfort zone, sitting pretty. It is when we are emotionally, mentally or spiritually violated when we have to use fear to our benefit.

Sometimes fear can be just what you need to spring yourself forward. It is unproblematic to become a victim of complacency, so God bestows a call to serve; a holy call for spiritual purpose and fulfillment. Fear can be used to excel you, kicking you out of your comfort zone so aggressively you cling to what you are familiar to. What you are most afraid of is your purpose. What you are most reluctant to complete, most afraid to move forward with or without, procrastinate the most about, what you are most affected by is directly connected to your divine purpose. My purpose of writing a book, detailing the ups and downs of a young Christian woman and a victim of a broken heart, I was deathly afraid of moving on without my ex. The direction of my life was completely depended on whether my ex and I were having a good or bad day. I was emotionally dependent on him, instead of on God. And the results clearly demonstrated where my heart was. I was afraid to find a life of my own, to actually confront what was hindering me. I allowed it to take over my life as I remained stagnant and unproductive.

Fear is always accompanied with confusion, insecurity and doubt. These qualities assist your refusal to submit your will to the will of Gods. Fear rears its ugly head only when you fail to trust God. You feel as if you must maintain control at all times; making every decision and executing choices you believe are best. The enemy of your soul will sadly attempt to keep you stuck in your past or present; looking backwards instead of looking to your greater achievements of the future. Since he can not hinder the destiny that awaits you, he relentlessly tries to keep your mind contemplating on what used to be. To instill fear, the enemy will present ifs, maybes, and should of, could of, would ofs. He'll offer up memories of the good old times, the happy times, who you used to be and the things you used to do to promote inactivity. He'll present negative thoughts that welcome feelings of doubt. But how could you possibly move forward if you are constantly looking back? How could you meet God half way, reaching out to grab hold to His hand, if your focus is turned around opposite from Him? It's simple. You can't. It's not possible to trust God while wanting something God doesn't want. When the Holy Spirit dwells in your heart, you begin to adjust. Your hearts desire will begin to line up with the will of God. During my time of self-renewal after my breakup, I was praying for a revelation, for a brand new start, for inner renewal...all while looking back. I was attempting to return to the very thing God took away. I was looking for life in death. I was relentlessly searching for light in darkness. My heart was chasing a heart that had ran far away from me.

The Bible describes what happened to Lots wife in Genesis 19:25-26, "And he overthrew those cities, and all the plain, and all the inhabitants of the cities, and that which grew upon the ground. But his wife looked back from behind him, and she became a pillar of salt." Genesis 19:17 (NLT) reads, "When they were safely out of the city, one of the angels ordered, "Run for your lives! And don't look back or stop anywhere in the valley! Escape to the mountains, or you will be swept away!" God specifically instructed them to flee, unless they be consumed with death. Lots wife chose to look back, when she was instructed not to. When she did, she became a pillar of salt, because she could not leave the past as exactly that, the past. Be very mindful of the tricks of the enemy against your mind. Your testimony, lessons learned and new found wisdom are the only advantages to looking back, and that is only temporary and short lived to share your testimony for Gods glory. The past is not designed to be a mental playground, but as a springboard to bigger and better. Never take a step back! Do not allow fear to hinder you, it is not of God. As you make a habit of praying about everything, talk to God about what you are fearful about. Fight fear with trust. Fight the potential stronghold of anxiety and fright with faith and courage. Lightness always overcomes darkness. The way, truth and light of God will always conquer any weapon the enemy forms against you, including fear. Any feelings of fright are direct tell-tell signs of the enemys frustration with what he can not change. He knows what the Lover of your Soul has prepared for you, and he attempts to inflict a feeling of uncertainty and insecurity to keep you in bondage. When you fight fear with faith, you will always win!

MISS THANGS LIFE QUOTE:

"The only time you take a step back is to get a better look at the path ahead."

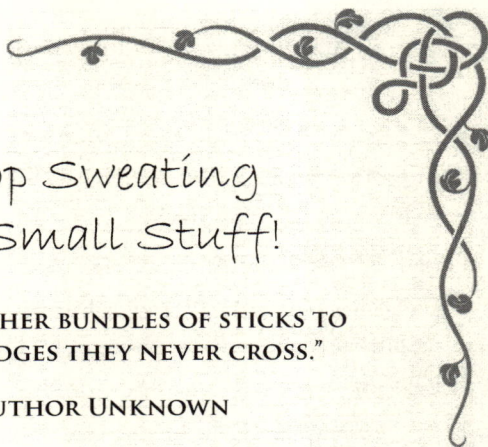

Stop Sweating the Small Stuff!

"PEOPLE GATHER BUNDLES OF STICKS TO BUILD BRIDGES THEY NEVER CROSS."

~AUTHOR UNKNOWN

Sistas, it's time for you to stop sweating the small stuff! It is time for you to start picking your battles and start taking control over your lives! Order can not co-exist with chaos and emotional clutter. It is time to stop allowing every little thing rob you of your joy! A key quality of *Miss Thang* is not being easily angered. It is time to stop opening unwanted doors and ushering in any annoyances that steal your peace! It's time to start guarding your heart and mind, cautious of whom you allow in your inner circle. Jesus stressed this point in Proverbs 4:23 (NLT), "Guard your heart above all else, for it determines the course of your life." God knows the importance of guarding your heart with vigilance, because out of it flows the spring of life. It is what is in your heart that determines your thoughts, words, actions and motives. If your heart is brimming with love and mercy, love and mercy will be reflected in your actions and reactions. This includes how you react to varying circumstances that occur on a daily basis.

It is time to stop sweating the small stuff! There is no need to cry over spilled milk! There is no need to worry about your spiritual fight, for the battle is not yours. Exodus 14:14 explains, "The Lord shall fight for you, and ye shall hold your peace." There is no need to worry when God is on your side! "The LORD is my light and my salvation--whom shall I fear? The LORD is the stronghold of my life--of whom shall I be afraid?" (Psalm 27:1 NIV). Work on your relationship with yourself and become more spiritually mature. When you are spiritually ripe, your faith is like a rock. Your peace and joy is not easily moved, and you face battles head on as God intercedes on your behalf. Just like the story of David and Goliath. With the help of God, David was able to defeat a giant, but the victory can only occur when you allow God to fight for you and with you.

Life is full of inconveniences. There will always be something going on in your life in one aspect or another that is not favorable. Countless are the times during the day opportunities presented to you are upsetting and frustrating, that disappoint you and attempt to steal your joy. A good attitude and a lifestyle that mirrors God's instruction is imperative to overcome any obstacles thrown your way. You must decide to walk in victory. Happiness is a decision. When you wake up in the morning, you must decide to not allow anything to steal your joy. You must surrender yourself to the Lord everyday, slaying your flesh so that you are in the center of His will at all times. When you give your day to the Lord, you are already keenly aware that whatever happens throughout the day, and whatever does not happen throughout the day works for your good. John 16:22 reads, "So with you: Now is your time of grief, but I will see you again and you will rejoice, and no one will take away your joy." What a scripture! Jesus Himself tells you that you will indeed rejoice, and live with joy that surpasses all understanding. So that regardless of what you go through, your peace and bliss are secure; firmly planted in the security that is Christ. The world did not give you the joy you have, so the world can not take it away. The world cannot close a door that God has opened. Nothing can counteract the works of God, nothing can take away your joy unless you allow it to. God is looking out for you in every aspect of your life. God has your back! When you live this truth, toxic people, unsettling situations, disappointing circumstances, and negative words will roll off your back. When you live in the truth that God directs your steps, your elation and coveted tranquility is stable. God gives you His peace and His strength in your weakness to deal with anything and everything possible.

"Peace I leave with you; my peace I give you. I do not give to you as the world gives. Do not let your hearts be troubled and do not be afraid" (John 14:27 NIV). This is one of my favorite verses in the Bible. God lets us know that there is no need to be afraid, for He is the master of this world, and everything is under His control; "These things I have spoken to you, so that in Me you may have peace. In the world you have tribulation, but take courage; I have overcome the world." (John 16:33). It is a decision whether we allow ourselves to be troubled. We are given a choice whether we allow certain situations, people and circumstances encourage fear and enable a troubled mind. That is why it's crucial to lean on Him at all times. Jesus is your burden bearer! He wants you to casts all of your fears to Him, for He knows all about each one. There is nothing that He does not understand, there is nothing that He can not relate to. Right now, right here, make the conscious and willful decision to refuse to let anything or anyone rob you of your joy, but instead live a fulfilled, jovial life. All you have to do is learn to be glad exactly where you are, and God will do the rest. When you lean on Him, the same God will get you where you want to be.

Don't allow temporary people to have a permanent effect on your life. People are a part of one of the three periods; for a season, reason, or lifetime. Take an inventory of everyone and everything in your life and allow the Holy Spirit to discern the category in which they apply. Prepare yourself ahead of time; the Holy Spirit may reveal something you don't want to believe! He knows the true hearts of people around you. It is time to start celebrating the end of things, including relationships, business deals, careers, personal habits, jobs, friendships, etc.! An ending of one thing is the ideal setup for a new beginning. What is failing to exalt you should be dropped! But, "Angela, whatevers worth having is worth fighting for, right?" you ask. Yes, but only to an extent. Of course you should work hard for whatever you desire, but when the bad begins to outweigh the good, that's a sign. It's a reason that everything happens or does not happen. There is not one detail that slips through the hands of God. Rejection is God's protection. That protection is God's provision. If you are fighting for something, honestly ask yourself why exactly are you fighting? Recognize whether you are truly trying to squeeze a square shape into a circular opening. There is a reason for strife between you and another person, there lies a divine motive much bigger than you, so be cautious of moving forward continuing in circles. Whatever God wants you to do, it's accompanied by a calming peace, comfort and security. Do not, however, confuse peace with easiness. What God instructs you to do or endure will not always be effortless, unproblematic or trouble-free. It is through those times you will have divine serenity and harmony; you won't question the situation.You will be at peace, regardless of the circumstances.

Remember, nothing is by accident! There is a reason that conflict is present. That is a clear indication of your heart fighting with what God says; and that is a big red flag. Nothing should take more from you than it gives. Some people are just not equipped to tag along with you to the Promised Land. Your destiny is too abundant, and God will not allow them to cleave to your coat tail. Are you clinging to what God is striving to take away? God sees what you can't; the heart, motive and mind. Trust Gods way instead of your own, and trust what God shows you about a person or specific matter. He is ALWAYS right. If you refuse to face it now, you will be forced to face it later. So why waste the time? You do not want to waste the next five years of your life chasing an illusion.

MISS THANGS LIFE QUOTE:

"If everything is always coming at you, you're probably in the wrong lane."

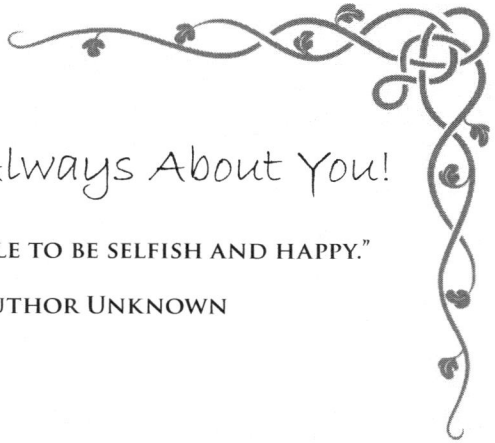

It's Not Always About You!

"IT'S IMPOSSIBLE TO BE SELFISH AND HAPPY."

~AUTHOR UNKNOWN

Are you familiar with the hip, upbeat gospel song by Bishop Noel Jones entitled, "*It's not about us*"? The first verse sings, "Its not about fame, you don't even have to know my name! It's not about us, but it's about Jesus!" That song was a great eye-opener to me and my walk with Christ. I came to realize that even the most minute and unimportant situations that occurred in my life were specifically by God's design. Nothing is by coincidence, nothing catches God off guard, for the journey was predestined. There may be times when what we go through will be specifically intertwined with someone elses destiny. We are not only blessed to have a life of abundance and ever growing fellowship, but we are blessed to be a blessing. God works on us to work through us. God will use us and His resources to help someone else in need. As mom always says, "Hindsight is always 20/20." Isn't it amazing how clearly you see when your position changes, when you're on the outside looking in? God allowed me to endure a painful heartbreak to be a witness! My purpose and passion is to share how God rescued me in my time of need and to help someone who is going through what I did. Through the course of my healing, God drew me closer to Him. And it was all by design. What we think is a failure, is actually the perfect setup! When we think we lost the world, that's when God steps in to show us how our past cannot compare to our future!

Whenever I think of this revelation, I want to cry. When I was little, I loved to write stories. You could not pull my notebook from my hand with the jaws of life! To this day I have boxes full of notebooks, completed with my short stories, poems, movie scripts and even soap opera dramas! God blessed me with a keen desire and natural talent to write. As I matured, my passion for writing decreased, and I wrote it off as a temporary childhood phase. Writing became a thing of the past the moment I discovered makeup, hip hop and boys! It wasn't until I re-discovered God, from a totally different perspective did God usher me full circle, gave me a new beginning and brought my writing dream to reality. Gods perfect plan brought me back to writing, but this time, with a praise on every written word and a sweet, sweet anointing on every page. It was all apart of the plan! As a child, God blessed me with a gift, and He now uses my gift to share the glory and saving grace of Jesus. Who knew I would have written a book, especially about this! God has given you a natural talent, too! Something you do so great you don't have to try. Something that comes as second nature, something that you do so well no one living, dead, or yet to be born can do as good as you! What is it? God wants to use it for His glory!

God uses His people to help bring salvation to others. And I, Sistas, am one of those people, and so are you if you want to be! My story is so unique because everyone saw my pain, and everyone knew my business- actually they knew more about my situation than I did! Those two years were the darkest years of my life, and the city of Columbus, Ohio had a front row seat, equipped with VIP passes and all access passes to boot! But what the devil meant for bad, Jesus meant for good all along. Afterward, I realized my journey was not about me. He used that valley I was subjected to in order to save a teenage girl from making the same mistakes I did. My valley was for that young woman who is also hurt, and who can relate to my story. After reading my testimony, she'll give her life to Christ and be saved. She'll have hope! She'll know that pain doesn't last always! She'll know that this too shall pass. It wasn't about me all along, but it was about God and His kingdom.

While writing this book, the Lord put on my heart, *"Everyone saw your pain, but now everyone will see your success."* What a promise! God never fails to turn what was designed to defeat me into something that exalted me. Valleys are overflowing with purpose. Challenges are filled with character crafting, diligence, and resilience, for we are meant to overcome! We are survivors and conquerors, wear it proudly! I am not ashamed of what I went through, because I would not be where I am if I did not endure it. If I would have taken my own life, my son and my family would be without me, completely devastated by my decision fueled by anger and hate. At the time, I did not know who God was, so I did not understand anything I went through. I felt picked on, like I was being bullied during grammar school recess. I screamed to the high heavens, "Why God?! Why me?!", until God politely and sincerely responded with, "Why not you?" I was not screaming and praising God in that trial because I actually blamed God. I blamed Him every time I had to see the neighbor my fiancè impregnated and had an affair with twice a day, even sharing a backyard with her! Our kids attended the same daycare center! We were both members of the same clubs! I am thankful more than ever for everything I went through. When I look back, it was all apart of the plan! The Word tells us, "The mind of a man plans his way, but the Lord directs his steps" (Proverbs 16:9

NASB). My steps were specifically ordered by God and I thank Him everyday.

It is similar to the pain of childbearing. The excruciating pain of contractions seem so unbearable, but the beautiful birth of the child is breath taking. My pain birthed my purpose; to help other women who have been in hurtful relationships and to live a life of greatness. And that, Sistas, made it all worth it. If I could change just one woman's life with this book, every tear I cried and every sleepless night I experienced would have been worth the torment. I have realized that it wasn't about me all along, and its not about you either. We are all God's vessels. God works through us. Everything we do should glorify the Lord. "I will bless the Lord at all times, His praise shall continually be in my mouth" (Psalm 34:1).

God wants to use you, too! Even through your successes and your achievements, He uses us, not just through our pain. Anyone who knows me knows that it was nothing but God working in my life. Nothing. But. God. He worked so phenomenally that nothing can steal Gods shine! No one else is due the credit but God. I was so low, so hurt, so beaten, so down and broken that it could only be God who restored me. God illustrates His mercy and greatness and love through healing. He gets all the glory. So when trials comes, He is also using you to witness to others. He wants you to share what He did for you, because He didn't have to deliver you. He didn't have to bring you out and bring you up. He chooses to because He loves you that much. He wants you to show everyone His glory by the work He did with you! Will you let Him?

MISS THANGS LIFE QUOTE:

H.O.P.E. ~ Having One Purpose Everyday

If You Don't Have Anything Nice To Say...

(WELL, YOU KNOW THE REST!)

~MOMS FROM AROUND THE WORLD

Mom was unquestionably on to something when she would say to us as kids, *"If you ain't got nothing nice to say, don't say nothin' at all!"* This philosophy not only applies to hurting someone feelings, but it also speaks of the power of our words over our own lives. Words are so powerful. They can either speak love, positivity and life, or they can do the exact opposite. The power of the tongue is so significant, it's unfathomable! Most people are unaware of the power they possess between their two lips. The Word provides us with numerous verses on the power of the tongue,

"For the Scriptures say, If you want to enjoy life and see many happy days, keep your tongue from speaking evil and your lips from telling lies." 1 Peter 3:10 NLT

"Gentle words are a tree of life; a deceitful tongue crushes the spirit." Proverbs 15:4

"If you claim to be religious but don't control your tongue, you are fooling yourself, and your religion is worthless." James 1:26

"Likewise the tongue is a small part of the body, but it makes great boasts. Consider a great forest set on fire by a small spark." James 3:5 NIV

"And the tongue is a flame of fire. It is a whole world of wickedness, corrupting your entire body. It can set your whole life on fire, for it is set on fire by hell itself." James 3:6 NLT

"It is not what enters into the mouth that defiles the man, but what proceeds out of the mouth, this defiles the man." Matthew 15:11 NASB

"But the things that proceed out of the mouth come from the heart, and those defile the man." Matthew 15:18 NASB

Need I say more? Oh, the power we hold with our tongue! The best example of the authority of the tongue is God Himself, and how He simply *spoke* the world into existence! "And God *said*, 'Let there be light,' and there was light" (Genesis 1:3). He did not create the world with His hands, feet, or with an army of elves. God spoke what He wanted into existence. Psalm 33:6 (ESV) tells us, "By the word of the LORD the heavens were made, and by the breath of His mouth all their host." *By the word of God*, did you miss it? How about this one. "For He spoke, and it was done; He commanded, and it stood fast" (Psalm 33:9 NASB).

Our words are spirits. "Sticks and stones may break my bones but words will never hurt me" has never been so far from the truth! Words are verbal energy- and emotion resonating itself into words.

Words create feelings, verbalize emotions, spew positivity, negativity, life or death. What are you using your vocabulary for? Are you using your tongue to speak life into a friend who is down and out or are you spreading her private information she entrusted you with? Are you gossiping? Are you lying? Have you ever experienced a situation where you said something, and immediately after you spoke you wish you could take it back? That's because language is like a sword. Our words can act as seeds of life and encouragement, or they can cut deep like sharp knives.

I am convinced the universe has a sense of humor! Just as we use our words unruly in the lives of those around us, our words actually apply to our very own life as well! It always manages to award us exactly what we speak. Call it a self-fulfilling prophesy. As we speak our words, the universe assumes that if we said it, we must want it. I'm always fascinated by women who say '*all men are dogs*', or, '*all the good ones are taken*', then wonder why they're single. They speak negativity and wonder why negativity is all they receive. The popular response, '*I'm stressed!*' to the question of how one is doing is nothing less than a setup for a setback! They wonder why they don't have any victory in their lives after they self proclaim they are indeed stressed! They literally call the stress 24 hour hotline every time they acknowledge stress and speak on it. Life will make sure you stay stressed as long as you speak it. I hear all too often how '*broke*' people are and lacking financial solidity, but speaking those words calls it into reality. Rest assured, there it is, Mr. Broke, on the fast track to your bank account, making sure you get exactly what you professed! Because your words manifest first with a thought, you must take a mental inventory everyday. For what comes out of your mouth is what is in your heart. A common excuse to spiritual questioning and conviction is, *"Well, God knows my heart!"* Yes, He does, and so do I, because your words and actions are clear reflections of just that...your heart.

Start speaking life into your own life. Start encouraging yourself, esteem yourself, congratulate yourself and pat yourself on the back for a job well done at the end of a hectic work week. I challenge you to speak nothing but positive words, giving a smile to every living creature you meet and refuse to complain about anything for one whole week. I dare you. I dare you to challenge your words. Refrain from gossip. Refrain from complaining about what you don't have, the man you do or don't have, the job you hate, the money you lack, and everything else that doesn't tickle your fancy. If you can monitor your words for just one week, I guarantee you will begin to notice a positive difference in your relationship with yourself, others, and God. Happiness and joy will follow you every day you do so.

To Fly!:

To be Refined, Fresh, Polished, Superior, Worthy, Lavish, Prime, Graceful, Posh, Classy, Upright, Distinguished, Delightful, Top Notch, Valued. To reflect internal and external attractiveness.

Miss Thang! Is High Quality.

Being Weak So God Can Be Strong

"IF YOU CAN'T FLEE IT, DON'T FIGHT IT, JUST FLOW WITH IT!"

I t is imperative to know that God cannot fill full hands. That philosophy was something I had to learn the hard way. God could not be intimate with me and teach me and show me how to please Him while I was pre-occupied trying to please someone else. The Bible says, "...seek ye first the kingdom of God, and His righteousness, and all these things shall be added unto you." (Matthew 6:33 NKJV). Think about that. You must seek God first, then He will fulfill your desires accordingly. He knows exactly what He's doing, for He sees what we can not see. He sees the bigger picture, while we only see what may happen in the next hour, which isn't guaranteed either. God wants to be number one in your life; He wants to be your everything and more! So whatever you are idolizing, God may choose to withhold it from you because He wants to be your first love. Only God can fill any type of void you may experience. Jesus is an ever present help, a constant friend is He! Which is why it is essential to learn how to be weak. Yes, you read it right! You must learn how to be weak in Him, because Jesus is all the strength you need! The Bible says, "My grace is sufficient for you, for power is perfected in weakness." Most gladly, therefore, I will rather boast about my weaknesses, so that the power of Christ may dwell in me." (2 Corinthians 12:9 NASB). Just writing that makes me want to shout! Regardless of what we go through, in times of trouble, if your grip gets weak, Gods grasp gets tighter. It is when you are at your weakest is when God is at His strongest!

When you are confused or dwelling too hard or too long about an issue, it is bigger than you, and is not designed for you to fight. It is designed to simply endure it with the strength of God and rest in his perfect peace. It's too big for you to handle, it's Gods battle, and God assures us that we already have the victory! Remember you do not have to fight. The devil has been defeated! Turn whatever you are going through over to God. He already knows your needs before it is even needed. Your steps are perfectly ordered, and before a situation even has the opportunity to present itself, the problem has already been solved. Angels were sent on your behalf to work it out in advance. And in those heart breaking times when it feels as if you can not pray, allow your tears to pray on your behalf. Tears are liquid prayers. Your tears are so important to God. They express your true feelings and any buried pain, forcing it to reveal itself. Tears is weakness escaping the body. Let them flow and let it go.

For strong spiritual stability, you must surrender to God. Put everything out in the open. God longs to be your friend! He is your confidant. The one who knows you better than you know yourself. The one who looks out for you even when you fail to look out for yourself. The one who is faithful to you even when you disobey Him. He is your BFF; best friend forever. In Him, you can be vulnerable. Although He is the Almighty God, the only one who is perfect in all His ways, and can judge you accordingly, He does not. He wants to have a relationship with you, He wants to show you who He is, but how can He if you never give Him a chance?

You must learn how to be weak in Him, to depend on Him without a second thought or doubt. His unchanging hand loves you unconditionally and He desires for you to lean on Him for all your cares. He is eager to work out your problems, but you have to give them to Him. You do not have to be Superwoman, for who needs to be when you have Jesus? "If God is for us, who can be against us?" (Romans 8:31). What is there to worry about when you are a daughter of the Almighty King? When you are in the center of His palm, His perfect will, everything you experience is for your good. EVERYTHING! It's amazing how God transforms failures into successes and your trials into triumphs. Make it a habit to trust God and lean on Him for all your needs.

Why worry when God makes the impossible possible? Why worry when God can make a way out of no way? Why worry when God can use what Satan tried to use for bad and turn it into good? Through my own personal experiences and maybe through yours, I have realized just how much trust God actually has in me. God never places too much on us, even though at times we may think God has somehow gotten our strength and ability confused! God sees our potential, He sees the strength in us that we do not even see in ourselves. He loves us for where we're going and not for where we're at.

God never asks us to do anything without giving us the resources and grace to do so successfully. For instance, God instructs us to love our neighbor, so yes; we have the grace of God to do what He asks. God has tremendous faith in us! Make it a habit to lay your burdens down before the Lord. He's waiting patiently with open arms for you! God has so much prepared for us that He even told us, "No eye has seen, no ear has heard, no mind has imagined, what God has prepared for those who love Him." (1 Corinthians 2:9 NLT). Difficulties in life are not meant to break us down, but to build us up. After all I had been through, I blamed God. Surely I pointed the finger at God because He could have stopped my ex's infidelity. He let this happen to me! I now realize it was for the best, and now I have peace that passes all understanding. The pain and heartbreak that I experienced brought me closer to Jesus. He was my strength when I was weak. He was my rock when I was in sinking sand. He was my friend when friends left me. He demonstrated His unconditional love through the disappointment of others.

The Lord was my anchor, my rock, my ever present help, security, and comforter. Past memories strive to make me turn backwards, looking toward what I used to be instead of where I'm going. In times of insecurity, you must encourage yourself, because God did not bring you this far to let you down. The same God that brought me through can do the same thing for you, too! If He can deliver me from a mind scattered with suicidal thoughts, broken heart, dead hopelessness, and a defeated attitude, He can definitely bring you out of whatever you may be going through.

There were times when I wished that I could forget what I went through: the utter embarrassment, shame, guilt, hatefulness and pain. God, however, does not want me to forget because that is my testimony. I know what it feels like to be completely broken. I am thankful more than ever, and I cling even tighter to Him because I know where he brought me from and what He has done for me. I know who I used to be, and when God saved me He made me into a new person. Everything of the past has been forgiven and forgotten and God has truly given me a new start. Before I allowed the actions of others to keep me in bondage. But God chose me before I was formed in my mothers' womb and pre-destined me for greatness. His favor was upon my life before my birth, as He pursued me, rescued me, loved me, cared for me, and guided me into my perfection!

We are all divine originals, fashioned by God to be radiantly beautiful, but I am still blemished. God knows that. That's why He never gives up on me. The feeling of unforgiveness and resentment lying heavily on my heart was a stepping stone into my future, into my perfectly planned future. Through it all He has restored me, and ensured me that it's okay to cry and be vulnerable in Him. God "...keeps track of all my sorrows. He has collected all my tears in His bottle. He has recorded each one in His book" (Psalm 56:8 NLT). God does not like to see His children cry, so much so He keeps our cried tears as keepsakes, determined to turn our blemished X's into crosses.

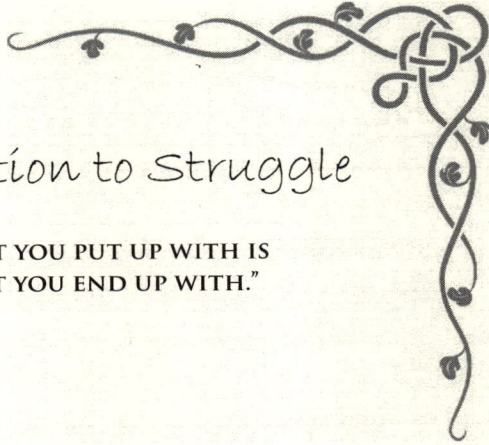

The Option to Struggle

**"WHAT YOU PUT UP WITH IS
WHAT YOU END UP WITH."**

It is a well known fact that people struggle everyday. Some people have actually become so comfortable with their struggles that they hang up pictures, grow plants, and throw parties, all in the midst of their misery! A few months ago my pastor made an interesting comment during Sunday service, "If some people were to wake up without any struggles, they'd think they were dead!" What a revelation it is to know that struggling is optional. Yes, optional! We all have challenges, but struggling is a way of life, a chosen lifestyle, and a way of thinking, so to speak. God's Word tells us, "No weapon that is formed against you shall prosper" (Isaiah 54:17 NASB). Read it closely. It does not say a weapon will not form, because they will, but that they will not break you, only escalate you. Anything that was created to break you and take you out didn't work! You made it! If you are currently experiencing a storm, you will make it! You can survive whatever life throws in your direction! God will not allow your enemies or spiritual forces to break you down. It is the lingering aftermath; the bitterness, anger, confusion and vengefulness that is a conscious choice you must reject. It's all up to you. It's how you deal with your challenge is what makes all the difference.

After I finally came to my senses and realized that I could not go back to my cheating fiance` and childs father, I was very angry, bitter and hurt beyond measure. Hurt more than you could ever possibly know. People who I thought were my friends talked about me more than my haters did! I was left all alone, or so I thought. I was attempting to solve my own problems and heal my own hurt and pain. And of course, to no avail; falling flat on my face every time I tried, until the Lord showed His face to me; He heard my cry, healed my pain and put my broken heart back together. Even to this day, memories tend to reappear, never failing to remind me of the mistakes I made and how I wasn't good enough. But whenever my past tries to hinder my future with plaguing memories, I simply call on the name Jesus. There's power in that name! God says we don't have to shout, we don't have to scream His name, because when you call Him, He's already there. He already knows, and is ready and willing before the call. Whether I'm in my car driving, showering, eating or listening to a song that reminds me of my past relationship, simply saying the name Jesus instantly eases my heart. The name of Jesus is the ultimate and free therapy!

He knows my weakness and my uncanny knack to mentally and emotionally travel backwards and dwell on what used to be, so He is a steady, ever ready help in my time of need. It has been a journey and it had took me years to move on. Throughout those years, the Lord has been working with me; showing me how to love, how to forgive others, including myself, and how to be the change in the world that I want to see. The journey has been a humbling, hurtful and helpful, but the Lord has never left my side. The Lord has been nothing but the perfect gentleman to me, and He can be for you, too! He gave me everything I lost, and He's still not done with me! He's not done with you either, Sista! This is only the beginning! He is just getting started. Make a conscious decision to not linger on the past.

Be encouraged that late in the midnight hour, God's going to turn it around, and it's going to work in your favor! I am truly a living witness to the glory of God! Challenges are guaranteed to come, but with God you will survive every last one of them. People will disappoint you. People will let you down, but does it matter who hurt you when God is able to heal you? Does it matter who lied on you when our God is bigger than your employer? Isn't our God bigger than any circumstance you could ever go through? Doesn't the Word of God overrule the doctor reports? Does it matter who hates you when God will make your enemies your footstool? Does it matter what your bank account says when our God made a promise to meet all our needs? Is there anything to hard for Him? Is there anything He can not do? Yes! There is one thing, and its fail. Start acting like Jesus is bigger than any struggle, and meditate on it. Pain doesn't last always, Honey!

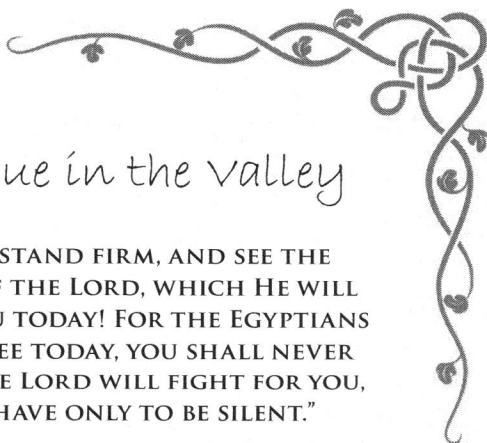

The Value in the Valley

"FEAR NOT, STAND FIRM, AND SEE THE
SALVATION OF THE LORD, WHICH HE WILL
WORK FOR YOU TODAY! FOR THE EGYPTIANS
WHOM YOU SEE TODAY, YOU SHALL NEVER
SEE AGAIN. THE LORD WILL FIGHT FOR YOU,
AND YOU HAVE ONLY TO BE SILENT."

EXODUS 14:13-14 ESV

B efore you skip this chapter, allow me to explain! Throughout this journey called life, you must learn how to embrace the tunnels and be thankful for your valleys. Everyone has issues, so it is not about the existence of the problem. The power is in the way you deal with your tests. Trials are the least bit enjoyable, but they are indeed required and inevitable. But behind your biggest storm lies your biggest miracle. After your most troubling trial is waiting your most triumphant blessing. Whenever you experience a challenge it's because God is attempting to get your attention! He wants to bring you into a closer relationship with Him! Think of a challenge as Gods wake up call. That means you are on His mind! He is thinking about you and wants to do more for you! Your trials mean upgrade, growth and divine advancement! In order for you to be closer to God, something has to be purged from your life, sometimes by hurtful means depending on how obedient you are. Usually the one thing you refuse to let go of is the one thing that's causing you the most damage. (See Idols). These things hinder your relationship with Jesus. We sometimes fail to take heed to warning signs, opting to move forward, leaning on our own understanding and reasoning instead of Gods. This always leads to trouble. Always. If it is not of God, it is not for you. God will not let you finish something He didn't start! His Word clearly tells us, "Trust in the Lord with all thine heart, lean not on your own understanding, but in all your ways acknowledge Him, and He shall direct thy paths" (Proverbs 3:5). When we are not in the perfect will of God, God gets our attention. He places obstacles in our paths so we can seek Him. If we only call on the name of the Lord when something goes wrong, God will keep us in "wrong" situations just so we can talk to Him! That's how much He wants to fellowship with you.

In order to be successful through your valleys, you must face change in the face and accept it and heed to it. Besides, change is inevitable. Whether you are ready or not, everything is subject to change. Nothing in your life is safe. Nothing is guaranteed, except for God. God is unchanging; He is the same as yesterday, today and tomorrow, and forever more- because when this life is over and you have nothing left, there will be God. Everything else will perish, but God is forever. I encourage you to hold on to His unchanging hand, especially through those changing times when His strength is made perfect. Without change you can not and will not be successful. Period. For example, you may desire a promotion on your job, but that promotion equals new responsibilities, duties, assignments and requirements. Although you have more responsibility, you have more rewards, too. The Word says, "to whom much was given, of him much will be required, and from him to whom they entrusted much, they will demand the more."(Luke 12:48 ESV). Oh yes! Change is bitter sweet, but necessary. Change is imperative, and through your trials you should change for the better, or you're destined to repeat them.

When your storm is completed, you are stronger, wiser, more aware and more trusting of God. You grow through what you go through. We all have challenges in life. It is not so much about the challenge itself, but how you deal with them. The lesson of a test is incredible! Until you learn the lesson, tests are oftentimes repeated until you upgrade spiritually and mentally. God wants you to "Be still, and know that I am God" (Psalm 46:10). You try so hard to be strong when instead God wants you to do the complete opposite and depend on Him. God despises independence! There is an all consuming comfort in having peace when you rely on God. You were not designed to fight strenuous battles. You were designed to cast away, trust in and lean on Jesus. He always takes care of the rest. If you have any doubt, ask yourself, has He ever let you down? Has He ever not provided all of your needs? I promise if you do your part, God will always do His. He never comes up short.

Valleys vary from financial issues, relationship and family concerns, to health problems to your career- but be encouraged! It will not be like this always! There will come a season of lack. Just as you rejoice in a season of reaping, you must also rejoice in a season of sowing and having less than. Through it all, you should strive to be like Paul in the Bible; "Not that I was ever in need, for I have learned how to be content with whatever I have."(Philippians 4:11 NLT).

Sometimes Jesus will allow unfavorable situations to occur to wake you up and to demonstrate His character to you. It's in those impossible situations where Jesus does His best work!

When you don't have a Plan B, a back up plan or a friend for support, God steps in like the strong tower that He is! Everything you go through has a specific purpose and works to your betterment. You have a divine purpose. I could not have written a book testifying of a shattered heart, a time when I was at my absolute lowest point after being embarrassed, deceived, cheated on, gossiped about, lonely, depressed and suicidal had I never experienced it. The purpose of the storm was to provide a storm testimony. This has become my ministry. I can express the glory of God even more so now than before. When you are in the midst of a storm and feel as if God has forgotten about you, remember:

The will of God will never take you:
Where the grace of God cannot keep you
Where the arms of God cannot support you
Where the riches of God cannot supply you
Where the power of God cannot endow you

The will of God will never take you:
Where the Spirit of God cannot work through you
Where the wisdom of God cannot teach you
Where the army of God cannot protect you
Where the hands of God cannot mold you

The will of God will never take you:
Where the love of God cannot enfold you
Where the mercies of God cannot sustain you
Where the peace of God cannot calm you
Where the authority of God cannot overrule for you

The will of God will never take you:
Where the comfort of God cannot dry your tears
Where the Word of God cannot feed you
Where the miracles of God cannot be done for you
Where the omnipresence of God cannot find you

~Author Unknown

Jesus wants to give you the desires of your heart, but His Word illustrates to us that, "No one puts new wine in old wine skins, or else the new wine will burst the skins, and it will be spilled, and the skins will be destroyed. But new wine must be put into new wine skins, and both are preserved. No man having drunk old wine immediately desires new, saying, The old is better" (Luke 5:37,38). God wants to change our very ways of thinking and reasoning, promoting us from basic understanding. He knows that we cannot upgrade our actions if our minds are not in agreement with the Word of God. If your heart desires a new home, your circumstances, way of thinking and lifestyle must change first. Your old, damaging habits and stinking thinking must cease. Jesus wants to bless you with a new car, but you have to be purged of the old car first. Show potential to the Lord that you can handle it, in addition to using it for His purpose to His glory. So, if you're riding the bus, know that God is preparing you for greatness!

Jesus desires to bless us; "And it is a good thing to receive wealth from God and the good health to enjoy it. To enjoy your work and accept your lot in life--this is indeed a gift from God" (Ecclesiastes 5:19 NLT). He delights in blessing His children; "I will certainly give you the wisdom and knowledge you requested. But I will also give you wealth, riches, and fame such as no other king has had before you or will ever have in the future!" (2

Chronicles 1:2). But He also wants to give us the means to accept and maintain the blessings, too! So when trials are presented, fight the urge to worry. Stay strong! Stand on the rock! Look toward the hills where your help comes from, for His hand is unchanging! God has you exactly where you need to be. You are in the perfect position for a spiritual promotion! Your steps are perfectly ordered, for nothing is out of place. Nothing surprises God. He is always thinking about you, and when you need Him the most, He is even more so on your side. You already have the victory! Your trials are a test of faith.

When your faith and obedience is being tested it is because God actually has tremendous trust in you! When trials appear you must know it is the beginning of the end of something toxic; an unneeded hindrance. "Trust in the Lord, with all thy heart, lean not on thy own understanding. In all thy ways, acknowledge Him, and He shall direct thy paths" (Proverbs 3:5-6). That, Sistas, is a promise! God knows your name, even through unfavorable situations, you are favored. Proverbs 3:16 tells us, "Long life is in her right hand; in her left hand are riches and honor". He wants to bless you abundantly, but first you must change in order to be in an appropriate position to accept it. God does not change your circumstances, He changes you in the midst of your circumstances. He does not stop the storms, the purpose of the storm is to perfect you through them. He wants you to get to know Him on a one on one basis through the valley, so embrace them and embrace Him.

Miss Thangs Life Quote:

"I will love the light for it shows me the way, yet I will endure the darkness for it shows me the stars."

~Og Mandino

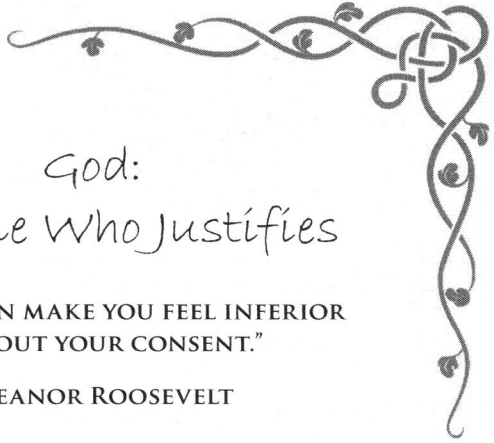

God:
The One Who Justifies

"NO ONE CAN MAKE YOU FEEL INFERIOR
WITHOUT YOUR CONSENT."

~ELEANOR ROOSEVELT

So often we look to others as a reference point to how we view ourselves. We unknowingly give our power away, allowing it to rest in the fickle and irrelevant opinions of others relating to our self worth. Instead of looking to the high heavens for acceptance and heavenly conviction, we look to our peers, family and friends for justification. Sometimes we make it a habit of looking in all the wrong places for love and acceptance. We look to everyone else and everywhere else than where we are supposed to look, to God. God is the ultimate justifier. He is the author of our lives, from the first page of our birth to the conclusion. We should all find our confidence, acceptance and advice through Him, and Him alone. If we fail to do so, our sense of self-worth and confidence will rise and fall, because they are totally dependent on what someone thinks.

Sistas, I urge you to find your peace in God, for He is the only one who can provide it. No one can take away what God provides. No one can close a door that God Himself opens, and no one can open a door that God Himself closes. When we rest in the perfect, all consuming glory of God, we walk and talk with an overwhelming sense of peace. We know that if we are accepted by Christ, the opinions and thoughts of another fails in comparison. I would rather be accepted by God and not accepted by the world than to be accepted by the world and not accepted by God. Mark 8:36 (NLT) asks, "What do you benefit if you gain the whole world but lose your own soul?"

The opinion of God is the only opinion that should matter. Pray to God to ask Him to reveal to you how He sees you. His opinions of us are faithful, constructive, loving and unbiased. He sees the best in us when everyone sees the worst. When everyone turns their backs on us, God draws in even closer to His children. He loves us more than anything and He demonstrates that love by showing us who He is: merciful, faithful, gracious, and forgiving. He is the best friend a woman could ever have! He does not criticize us, instead He gently convicts us of our wrong doing, urging us to repent so we can enjoy fellowship with Him again. His love is unwavering, because He is faithful to us through all of our mess: disobedience, idols, and sin. He is more faithful to us than we are to Him. He loves us when we don't love ourselves. He has our back when we don't have our own back. His love never fails. He also gives the best advice because He always has our best interest at heart. He knows what we can handle and what we can't. Besides, advice is what we ask for when we already know the answer but wish we didn't. Our questions are really answers in disguise.

They're times when we get so out of touch with our God, our behavior is so unattractive we wouldn't even want to put up with ourselves! If someone treated us the way we treat God we wouldn't give them the time of the day. When we attempt to "D.I.O.", or do it ourselves, we find ourselves deeper entrenched in more mess than where we started. But His love never fails. When we disappoint Him with sin and are separated from Him, but His ever present help picks us up when we fall. He rescues us and loves us even more knowing that we are broken and knowing in desperate need of Him. It is imperative to place your confidence in God, a God who is the same as yesterday, today, and forever more.

A Woman of Virtue

"DON'T COMPROMISE YOURSELF.
YOU ARE ALL YOU'VE GOT."

~JANIS JOPLIN

When you look in the mirror, what do you see? Do you see what God sees? Do you smile at your reflection, admiring every detail of your being? Do you know that you are a gem in Gods eye, a jewel in His crown that was created in His image? He even asked the question, "Who can find a virtuous woman? For her price is far above rubies" (Proverbs 31:10 NKJV). You are so precious! God does not intend for us to hurt. We subject ourselves to hurt trying to do it our way. From a personal stand point, God was my last priority in my past relationship and I was living like it too! My behavior was of the world, which was displeasing to God as my sin and disobedience drew us further and further apart. But He was watching over me, the entire time, loving me just as much, waiting patiently and faithfully for me to come to Him. Before I even knew Him, He loved me. Amen! I had possessed a fear of being alone, disliked and undesired. My opinion of myself was based on everyone elses opinion of me; the exact opposite of what Jesus thought of me. I felt being in an unhealthy, emotionally abusive relationship was justified because it was better than nothing. It was not until after all the pain did that I came to realize that the best man a girl could ever wish for was already there: the one who writes the songs for the birds to sing, the one who gives the roses their bright color, the one who tells the sea to stand on end! In Jesus, you want for nothing!

Jesus longs to be your friend. He longs to be close to you. As He watches over you in your sleep, He anticipates waking you up in the morning so the two of you can enjoy fellowship together! As women, we settle too easy, accepting less than what we are worth. We have to decide to forget what we want and go for what we deserve! God is all that we could ever need, but we may feel undeserving of His divine grace. Check your insecurities at the door. When I discovered the details of my ex's infidelity, my confidence plummeted to the lowest of lows. I felt useless, unattractive, abandoned and betrayed. I felt as if it was my fault. I did not feel good enough for him. I began to question myself, doubting my talent. My self worth was non- existent. I soon realized that it had nothing to do with me, and everything to do with him. It took years to realize this revelation, but glory to God for healing and restoration! God has truly given me back everything the devil stole from me ten fold.You have to remember that God will never hurt you. So if you have to decide between a relationship and God, remember you will never wake up one morning and hear God tell you He doesn't love you anymore. So choose wisely. You are the cream of the crop! Get to know yourself, as Christ reveals himself to you.

Ask God for a spirit of wisdom and keen understanding about the people, things, and circumstances that surround you. A wise man once said you can always recognize the love and respect one has for herself based on her relationships. Show me your friends and I'll show you your character. Show me your relationships and

I'll tell you your standards. When you truly love yourself, you will be amazed at the better decisions you make! It is all about self love, Sista! In addition to self-love, your external relationships are imperative to your mental, emotional, spiritual growth and well being. They have the potential to upgrade and exalt you, but they can also drag you down. As a daughter of the King, you must be aware of who God places in your life to support and guide you. This is a part of self discovery and what you are willing to deal with and what you are not willing to deal with. And it is when you learn more about yourself, everything about you will compliment your standards and best attributes , and help perfect the ones that are in need of improvement. Ask God to show you how He sees you as you take time to get closer to God, to gain knowledge about your Maker and to learn about who He truly is. You will discover how much He loves you, how much He adores you that He sent His only son to die...just for you. If you were the only person on this earth, Jesus still would have given His life for you. That's how much a woman of virtue means to Him. God showed me He can heal my broken heart, but I had to give him all the pieces.

God teaches self love through triumphs and trials. The moment you ask Him into your heart, professing Him as your Lord and Savior, God will begin to teach you your worth. He teaches you to lean on Him, to trust Him in any and all circumstances. Aside from His company, He shows you how to love your very own company, too! You enjoy time spent by yourself. And because you are not equipped to deal with average, you do not settle because the children of God are not called to fit in. You have been called to a higher moral code and an outstanding spiritual life. The path less traveled is usually the path of God, because it is down those paths of adversity and unconformity is where God shows His awesome power! The darkest tunnels reveal God's brightest light. When you can't see the light at the end of the tunnel is because you're not in the tunnel anymore. You have been bought with a price, too precious to deal with anything less than stellar. Proverbs 31:10-31 describes what makes a woman virtuous.

[10] "A wife of noble character who can find?
   She is worth far more than rubies.
[11] Her husband has full confidence in her
   and lacks nothing of value.
[12] She brings him good, not harm,
   all the days of her life.
[13] She selects wool and flax
   and works with eager hands.
[14] She is like the merchant ships,
   bringing her food from afar.
[15] She gets up while it is still dark;
   she provides food for her family
   and portions for her servant girls.
[16] She considers a field and buys it;
   out of her earnings she plants a vineyard.
[17] She sets about her work vigorously;
   her arms are strong for her tasks.
[18] She sees that her trading is profitable,
   and her lamp does not go out at night.
[19] In her hand she holds the distaff
   and grasps the spindle with her fingers.
[20] She opens her arms to the poor
   and extends her hands to the needy.
[21] When it snows, she has no fear for her household;
   for all of them are clothed in scarlet.

²² She makes coverings for her bed;
    she is clothed in fine linen and purple.
²³ Her husband is respected at the city gate,
    where he takes his seat among the elders of the land.
²⁴ She makes linen garments and sells them,
    and supplies the merchants with sashes.
²⁵ She is clothed with strength and dignity;
    she can laugh at the days to come.
²⁶ She speaks with wisdom,
    and faithful instruction is on her tongue.
²⁷ She watches over the affairs of her household
    and does not eat the bread of idleness.
²⁸ Her children arise and call her blessed;
    her husband also, and he praises her:
²⁹ Many women do noble things,
    but you surpass them all.
³⁰ Charm is deceptive, and beauty is fleeting;
    but a woman who fears the LORD is to be praised.
³¹ Give her the reward she has earned,
    and let her works bring her praise at the city gate."

A Proverbs 31 woman is rare and precious. She is kind, trustworthy, diligently going the extra mile to get the job done. She is wise, elegant, and worthy of praise. She is distinguished and honored. She heeds to Gods instruction to be "equally yoked" to whomever she befriends and courts because she is well aware that two people who walk together must first agree on the direction, (Amos 3:3). A Proverbs 31 woman is priceless.

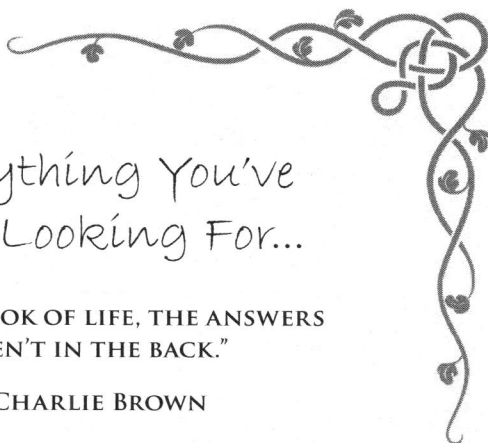

Everything You've Been Looking For...

> "IN THE BOOK OF LIFE, THE ANSWERS
> AREN'T IN THE BACK."
>
> ~CHARLIE BROWN

I s in Jesus! After looking everywhere for love, validation, acceptance and unconditional understanding, Jesus, our refuge and constant hand in the time of trouble, will always show up. He demonstrates to us exactly who He is and how He is. He is fully capable of filling any void in your life. That is how He created you! He created you to be in constant relationship and communication with Him. One of the many qualities of the Lord is how He understands you. He can relate to anything you feel. He knows exactly what you are going through. Jesus knows what it feels like to be betrayed, talked about, hurt and overwhelmed with great sorrow and loneliness. Matthew 26:48-50 (NLT) describes the betrayal of Judas, one of His twelve disciples; "The traitor, Judas, had given them a prearranged signal: 'You will know which one to arrest when I greet him with a kiss.' So Judas came straight to Jesus. 'Greetings, Rabbi!' he exclaimed and gave him the kiss. Jesus said, 'My friend, go ahead and do what you have come for.'

Then the others grabbed Jesus and arrested him." Although Judas was one of the closet men to Jesus, he betrayed Him. Judas was accompanied by a large crowd, all equipped with swords and clubs to seize, arrest, capture and send to death the one who claimed to be the Messiah. Jesus was betrayed in front of everyone! Betrayed by the very ones He came to save. The very ones who He was sent to fellowship with and share a relationship with refused Him. The very ones He came to spread the good news to persecuted Him, spit on Him and whipped Him without mercy!

Isaiah 53:3 describes how Jesus felt "…despised and rejected of Men; a Man of sorrows…". John 1:11 says, "He came unto His own and His own received Him not." Jesus felt loneliness! As He hung on the cross, He died all alone. Holding the sins of the world, He was apart from His Father: despised, unloved and hated by His own children. Jesus can relate to any pain you feel, for He has felt those same feelings. We can come to Him for anything and everything. He can carry all of our burdens if we lay them down at His feet. He is our burden bearer. His blood paid the price for us. Jesus knows what we can and can not handle and He is waiting for us to bring all of our needs to Him.

Isnt is refreshing to know that you are never alone? Isnt it refreshing to know that no matter what, you have a friend who sits on the right hand side of the throne of God? Isnt it refreshing to know that regardless of your circumstances, your God understands them all? Jesus was sent to this earth in an fleshly body to save us, so He is well aware of the tricks and temptations of the devil. Matthew 4:1-4 reads,

"Then Jesus was led by the Spirit into the desert to be tempted by the devil. After fasting forty days and forty nights, he was hungry. The tempter came to him and said,

"If you are the Son of God, tell these stones to become bread." Jesus answered, "It is written: Man does not live on bread alone, but on every word that comes from the mouth of God."

The tempter came to Jesus when He was hungry, attempting to use food as a reason to disobey God. Satan also tempts you at your weakest moment. When you are stressed, vulnerable and disappointed, the doors to your heart and mind are unlocked, allowing free entry and open reign. An idle mind is the devils playground. You must stay in prayer and constant communication with Jesus, for He knows what it is like to be tempted. Another example is in Matthew 4:8-11,

"Again, the devil took him to a very high mountain and showed him all the kingdoms of the world and their splendor. "All this I will give you," he said, "if you will bow down and worship me." Jesus said to him, "Away from me, Satan! For it is written: Worship the Lord your God, and serve him only." Then the devil left him, and angels came and attended him".

The devils desire is for you to serve him and not God. A clever trick of the tempter is to have us serve Him even without our notice or attention! As long as you are stagnant, the tempter is pleased! He does not mind your faithful attendance to church every Sabbath, because Monday through Saturday God is last thing on your mind. He does not mind you reading an occassional verse from the Bible, because if you are only a hearer of the Word and not a doer, you have not made any credible progress and your religion becomes useless and vain. The devils desire is for us to look away from God and look to the things of this world for satisfaction. Jesus was tempted by the devil to achieve His mission without the cross, but it did not work!

The devil knows when you are at your most vulnerable moment and he does not waste one second to capitalize on your insecurity. Be sure not to give the devil any opportunity to gain on your spiritual progress. You must be aware of the tricks of your enemy. His biggest trick is to convince you he does not exist. If you fail to even acknowledge him, he will use your ignorance against you. Ignorance is not bliss, it's fatal. Wisdom is imperative in your walk with Christ. In Ecclesiastes 7:12, "Wisdom and money can get you almost anything, but only wisdom can save your life." Hosea 4:6 (ESV) explains, "My people are destroyed for lack of knowledge…" The devil will use what you don't know or are in denial about, against you. A problem can never be solved if it is never addressed. Ignoring a problem unfortunately does not make the situation better. Instead it allows the underlying problem to fester, causing more damage.

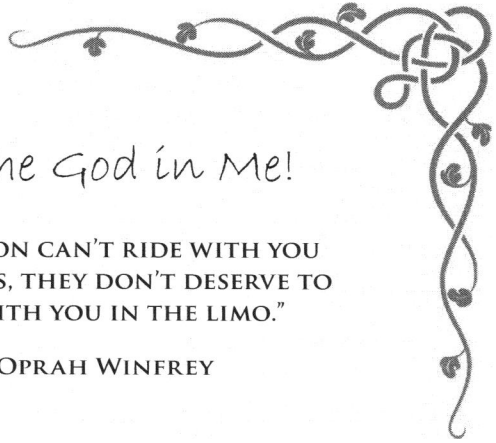

It's the God in Me!

"IF A PERSON CAN'T RIDE WITH YOU
ON THE BUS, THEY DON'T DESERVE TO
RIDE WITH YOU IN THE LIMO."

~ OPRAH WINFREY

The favor of God is noticeable. When a favored, distinguished woman of God walks into a room, believe me, everyone takes notice. Favor is attractive! Call it her swag that's so captivating that everywhere she goes, everyone wants to know! We are all Gods creation, but we are not all Gods children. "For many are invited, but few are chosen" (Matthew 22:14 NIV). God loves to show off His children. That is why you show the God in you more than you talk about the God in you. In addition to your actions, people will take notice to the joy you have, the peace you carry, how everything works out for you and how you win even when it seems you lose. Your peers will observe God's divine work in your life, thus, inspiring them to want to know more about what and who makes you this way. God will receive the glory from the work He does in your life.

People will be drawn to your spirit, which is why you must be ready to minister, testify, and share the joy of the Lord with anyone who may inquire. And you demonstrate His glory not only by your words and attitudes, but by your actions and lifestyle. Saying one thing and doing another are two totally different concepts. Do not claim the Christian title and live like a sinner Monday through Saturday. You cannot have your cake and eat it too! You are either living for God; following His commandments for kingdom living or you are living for the world. God calls His people out from the crowd; "Don't copy the behavior and customs of this world, but let God transform you into a new person by changing the way you think. Then you will learn to know Gods will for you, which is good and pleasing and perfect" (Romans 12:2 NLT).

Do not be a hypocrite! God sets you apart from the world. Hypocritical behavior gives a bad rep to the precious name of God and His kingdom. Claiming the name of Jesus but living as the world does stinks in the nostrils of God. He speaks of hypocrites in Revelation 3:15, "I know your deeds, that you are neither cold nor hot. I wish you were either one or the other!" God wants you to choose, hot or cold, the world or the kingdom of God. At least the atheists and humanists are honest with themselves. It is the person who thinks they are in good standing with God but really are the exact opposite is the most dangerous and confused. Deliberate conflicting words and actions is an insult to Christ; instead of planting spiritual seeds from God you sow into hypocrisy, and sinners looking for God will hesitate approaching you for guidance and advice. Recognize whether or not what you say is in tune with what you do. Are you only a hearer of the word, and not a doer (James 1:22)? You never know when Jesus desires to use you to help others. God blesses us to not only give us life, and live more abundantly (John 10:10), but He also blesses us to be a blessing. He uses His favor for His glory. He works to us and for us, to work through us.

In addition to sowing spiritual seeds, the favor of God also draws haters. If Jesus Himself was persecuted, talked about and lied about, then you will also experience this type of behavior. But do not be weary, people who talk about you reveal more about themselves than about you. You can always measure the amount of success one has by the pack of haters behind them! These people who do not want to see you succeed, people who speak negativity over your life, people who delight in your misfortune are snakes. Which is why you must be careful as to who you allow in your inner circle. *The one with drive always rides alone.* Everyone does not have a relationship with God, everyone does not follow His dictates. Everyone does not live by the same moral code that you may. Ask God for a spirit of discernment, so that you will become aware of anyone who does not have your best interest at heart.

MISS THANGS LIFE QUOTE:

"Be pushed by the ones who believe in you and motivated by those who don't."

The Importance of...

Recognize and acknowledge any doubts, insecurities and behavior that are not Christlike. It is essential to address any problems in your spiritual, emotional and mental foundation that may hinder your blessing and growth in Christ. In your spiritual walk, whether you are a babe in Christ or have been saved for 20 years, it is first imperative to recognize the importance of...

A.) CHARACTER

"IT'S FAR MORE IMPRESSIVE WHEN OTHERS DISCOVER YOUR GOOD QUALITIES WITHOUT YOUR HELP."

Character is defined as a distinguishing attribute or quality of an individual. It is a moral and ethical strength. In your walk with Christ, it is important to have character when dealing with people, yourself and your relationship with Christ. As you grow in Him, He grows in you. As you draw closer to God, He draws closer to you. The Holy Spirit begins to manifest Himself in your heart and you begin to exemplify the qualities of Christ. Jesus tells you in His Word in

John 14:9, "Anyone who has seen me has seen the Father." Honestly speaking, how many of you can say, "If you have seen me, you have seen Jesus?" Are your actions in line with the Word of God?

B.) MOTIVES

"YOU ARE WHAT YOU REPEATEDLY DO."

Proverbs 23:7 (KJV)reads, "For as he thinketh in his heart, so is he." This is such an important and loaded verse. It explains how what we think and what we give our heart and mind to are vital to our very existence. What is held in our heart, creates thoughts, which either produces productive, godly fruit or corrupted thinking, or what I like to call "stinking thinking." When our minds and hearts are not in tune with the Holy Spirit, it is reflected in our actions. Our hearts composition is revealed through how we treat people and how we treat ourselves. What is in our heart, the most ultimate, honest feelings, are directly connected to our motive. A motive is an emotional impulse as a result of whatever we think or feel. God knows the content of all hearts and He knows why you act or do not act the way you do. James 4:2-3 (NIV) explains, "You want something but don't get it. You kill and covet, but you cannot have what you want. You quarrel and fight. You do not have, because you do not ask God. When you ask, you do not receive, because you ask with wrong motives, that you may spend what you get on your pleasures."

When you go to God in prayer, making your requests known to God, first ask yourself why are you praying for that specific request. What is the true motive for your request? God Himself explains when you have ill motives or an unrighteous heart, you fail to receive your requests because your heart is unfit. Motives are rarely one hundred percent pure: fear, comfort, money, duty, guilt or reward are all factors that may alter a pure motive. It is when you have a spirit of competition, a spirit of complaining or a spirit of entitlement is when the very reasons why you ask for something becomes jaded. You are not spiritually, mentally, or emotionally prepared to receive the very thing you ask for. You lack spiritual maturity and a humble heart. God delights in providing His children their desires, but it is strictly conditional. God does not owe you anything. You are not due anything from Him. He will only provide what you can handle. He will not provide a blessing that will result as an obstacle. He will not provide a blessing that will result as an hindrance. God wants you to have whatever you can handle! It is up to you to work on yourself and to consistently work with God, to be in a place of humility and wisdom. God will provide all of your needs and then some when you have a pure heart; not looking to satisfy fleshly desires with prideful reasons.

C.) FAITH

F.A.I.T.H.-
FORSAKING ALL, I TRUST HIM.

James 2:17 (NLT), "So you see, faith by itself isn't enough. Unless it produces good deeds, it is dead and useless." Faith is the only way to please God! No alternative way exist to satisfy your Heavenly Father without unwavering faith in Him. Faith makes all things possible. Love makes all things easy. Good deeds, monetary charity donations and faithful church attendance every other day are great works indeed, but only your belief in Him is what truly pleases God. Faith is so important because it indicates your trust in Him. How does it make you feel when someone you love cannot trust you when you only have their best interest at heart? It is not a pleasant feeling.

You find yourself trying to prove your love and faithfulness to them. That is how God feels when you fail to trust Him, even though time and time again He makes a way out of no way. Even though He has never let you down and has provided all of your needs. Even though time and time again He bails you out of your mess, forgives you and gives you chance after chance after chance, your faith is still non-existent. How do you think that makes your Heavenly Father feel when He shows you His faith on a daily basis?

Your faith is not faith at all until it is tested by fire. One of my favorite verses from the Word is Song of Solomon 2:6, "His left arm is under my head and His right arm embraces me." This verse is extremely encouraging in the time of trouble when faced with adversity. As you grow in God, your faith grows deeper and you allow God and the Holy Spirit to work in your life completely. And because you know that all things work together for your good, through the most undesirable and uncomfortable circumstances you have peace and security. You grow when uncomfortable because you have no other choice but to change. You are forced to step out of your comfort zone.

When you are truly walking in faith, you know that your steps are ordered. Your faith in Him becomes second nature. His voice is recognizable to you and you heed to His every word because you know in the midst of a disobedient decision chaos is not far behind. You take calculated risks but look to Christ for every decision you make. Stop being addicted to what makes you comfortable. Jesus challenges His children to consistent growth, to a higher calling every season of your life. He dares you to place all hope and trust in Him. Those unwanted situations ignite fire on your bottom to chase you to His feet.

It is only those that can see the invisible are the ones who can do the impossible. It is those who release what's seen are those who receive the unseen. As Christians, we walk by faith, and not by sight (2 Corinthians 5:7). We must not look through our natural eyes but with our spiritual eyes. We must put our faith in God even when we can not see His work. With our natural eyes, we can not see the wind, but we know its there. This is the same as God. We must trust that Gods promises never return void. We must have unshakable faith that God goes before us making our crooked paths straight. Key word, *unshakable*. Faith is not faith on Sunday, doubt on Monday, worry on Tuesday, back to faith on Wednesday, with the rest of the week dependent on how your boss, boyfriend or friend acts or doesn't act! Your faith must be firmly grounded, despite what you go through.

Take the limits off of Gods ability and release the reigns of your life. *Brick walls exist to scare away those who don't want to win bad enough.* Allowing God to protect you, Jesus to guide you, and the Holy Spirit to lead you demonstrates complete trust and faith like none other. It only begins, however, when you surrender to Him. It is impossible to control your life and surrender to the will of God at the same time. When you pray, you do not answer the prayer for yourself. You do not pray with a previously determined outcome. Instead ask Gods will to be done and the strength to deal with His answer.

D.) YOUR PURPOSE

"HERE IS THE TEST TO FIND WHETHER YOUR MISSION ON EARTH IS FINISHED. IF YOU'RE ALIVE, IT ISN'T."
~RICHARD BACH

"Being confident of this, that He who began a good work in you will carry it on to completion until the day of Christ Jesus" (Philippians 1:6). In the hearts of Gods children, a light, a spiritual light, dwells in their souls. Whether this light shines or not, is a different story! This light represents your fruit bearing, your lifestyle, how you conduct yourself and treat one another. We all have a specific ministry or mission that God has assigned us. It's called our purpose. There is a reason why you were created on this earth, at this time, in the family and condition you were. Sorry! It was not by chance!

Aside from prayer, there is a method to determine what your purpose is. "For the Scripture says to Pharaoh: "I raised you up for this very purpose, that I might display my power in you and that my name might be proclaimed in all the earth" (Romans 9:17). God wants to use you for the kingdom of God, and you are the perfect candidate- flaws and all. His requirements do not include experience or a college degree, only your willingness. You do not need a list of references or approval from others. Jesus Himself highly recommends you! He is the ultimate endorser. Don't let small minds convince you that your dreams are too big. All you have to do is yield and surrender to God.

Everyone is assigned a divine purpose, a special gift or talent to spread the good news of Jesus. Your inner most dreams and most energetic, natural passion has shaped you and molded you into the very person you are today! The following questions will help you discover what your purpose is. Remember to be both objective and honest with yourself. There is no need to exaggerate your great qualities or diminish the ones in need of improvement. God already knows, anyway! Lying to yourself will only delay the process and possibly veer you off into a wrong and unnecessary direction.

1.) What do you give most to others?

2.) What do others look to you for the most?

3.) If money was not an object, what profession would you choose?

*4.) **What natural talents do you possess? What do you
do so well that practice is not required?***

*5.) **What are you most complimented on? Why do you
think that is?***

*6.) **What independent qualities were you born with?
(List both positive and negative qualities here. If
you are not good with kids, starting a childrens
ministry or working in a daycare is not for you!) Are
you a natural born leader? Do you have a knack
for details? Are you outgoing? Do you enjoy public
speaking or group assignments? Or are you shy and
reserved, preferring to work behind the scenes?***

*7.) **What specific group of people/demographic are you
most compassionate about? For example, runaway
teens, domestic abuse victims, fatherless sons, ex-
convicts, etc? Can you identify with the issues of
that demographic? Why?***

Your experiences and testimonies are directly connected
to your purpose. More often than not, you find yourself more
compassionate, more empathetic and more understanding toward
someone you can relate to. If you were once addicted to drugs
and God delivered you from the spirit of addiction, you were
spiritually impregnated with your purpose to minister to someone
who is still bound by alcoholism or drug abuse. If you were born
with a singing voice that rivals the morning songbirds, God wants
you to use your beautiful talent for His glory! Your voice and your
songs will be used as inspiration, and depression and spiritual
strongholds can be unyoked when you sing with the anointment
of God! Stow away to a quiet place for a spiritual self-evaluation.

Before you begin, pray that God reveals to you your purpose. After all, it is why you're here! Because if you don't execute your dreams, you will work the rest of your life working for someone who did!

MISS THANGS LIFE QUOTE:

"He who has nothing to die for has nothing to live for."

~Moroccan Proverb

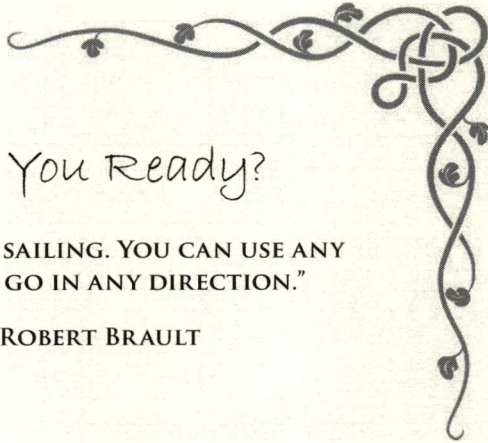

Are You Ready?

**"LIFE IS LIKE SAILING. YOU CAN USE ANY
WIND TO GO IN ANY DIRECTION."**

~ROBERT BRAULT

Just as you prepare in the morning for your day, Jesus is preparing you for a life filled with prosperity; both carnal and soul prosperity alike. He desires to provide you with both the health and the wealth, *as your soul prospers*. You may not be in the right position to receive your blessing, but be encouraged sista, it is on the way! Stay strong and do "not get tired of doing what is good. At just the right time we will reap a harvest of blessing if we don't give up" (Galatians 6:9 NLT). There is a time for everything, as there is a season for everything. Think about what season you are in. An easy way to complete a spiritual season inventory is to ask yourself whether you are reaping or sowing. In all situations, you are either sowing into your future or the future of someone else, or you are reaping the consequences of your own actions. This emphasizes the importance of how you treat one another because the theory of what goes around comes around and karma is actually biblical. God tells us in Romans 12:19, "Dearly beloved, avenge not yourselves, but rather give place unto wrath: for it is written, *vengeance is mine; I will repay, saith the*

Lord." Proverbs 20:22 also tell us, "Do not say, "I will repay evil"; Wait for the LORD, and He will save you." (See Chapter 3). It is time to get ready!

Take a moment to think of the beautiful flowers. The rotating seasons of the flowers are mere reflections of the seasons we experience in our very own lives. There is a time to reap and there is a time to sow. There is a season of abundance and a season of lack. In order to receive the blessings of God, you must be properly prepared, emotionally, mentally and spiritually. Lessons are often repeated until learned. You will travel through the same valleys, and jump through the same hoops until you wake up! Do better and be better! A fool is not someone who experiences problems, but someone who fails to gain the lesson from it. How long will you stay in your situation? Yes, God will allow trials to challenge and change us, but often times our undesirable situations are the result of our very own bad decision making! We all play the fool, but the real lesson is in how many times we choose to play it. How many times will you decide to be financially irresponsible? How many times will you be irresponsible with your heart and your time? How many times will you place God on the back burner for a relationship, career, material possession and various other forms of idols? How long will it take to look in the mirror and take responsibility for yourself and your children? It is time to stop meddling with stupidity and immaturity. It is time to get ready!

You must slay your flesh daily, every morning. When you wake up in the morning, I encourage you to speak a soft, "Thank you, Jesus" as the first words of the day. Give your day to God by surrendering your will to His perfect will. Your day will run a smooth course, despite any inconveniences or setbacks that is destined to occur. Your light will shine brighter and brighter; for Gods glory and for your good. Mentally prepare yourself to hear Gods gentle voice and emotionally prepare yourself for the blessings God has prepared for you! Keep your eyes wide open and be spiritually aware of your surroundings. Remain hopeful at all times! The children of God are always hopeful, readily expectant to receive the overflowing blessings of God. Get ready, Sistas! This is only the beginning! Your worst day with Jesus cannot even compare to your best day in the world. It is time to let God be God. Release Him from your box of limitations! He is not restricted by man, traditions, rules or religion. In life we experience disappointments which may taint our expectations, but praise be to God because He is not like who let us down before. With God "all things are possible" (Matthew 19:26). If an airplanes nose is pointed downward, it's about to crash, so stay fly! Are you ready to be fly, *Miss Thang*?

"For I know the plans I have for you," declares the LORD, "plans to prosper you and not to harm you, plans to give you hope and a future."

Jeremiah 29:11

References

NIT-New International Version
NLT-New Living Translation
NKJV-New King James Version
ESV-English Standard Version
NASB-New American Standard Bible
ISV-International Standard Version
KJV-King James Version

About the Author

From the tender age of 7, Angela always knew she was destined to be a writer. At age 10, when her first poem entitled "School Days," a short poem chronicling the hardships of the day in the life of an elementary school student, was published in the *Anthology of Poetry by Young Americans,* she knew she was on to something special! From movie scripts, daytime dramas to children books, Angela found her knack for writing in the solace of her childhood bedroom. She found a comfort and an incomparable joy when writing. Her notebooks became a fictional diary. As a mature writer, Angela caters to a female audience, sharing her heart and baring her soul with her readers with her upbeat and relatable writing format.

Angela tackles the tough issues of love, life and loss, and everything in between. After a 15 year hiatus from writing, Angela learned God does indeed work in mysterious ways! After rescuing her from an emotional all time low, transforming her, and making her over, Angela smartly heeded the instruction of God to tell the world what He had done for her. Thinking writing was just a childhood hobby, God brought her back to her first love: her pen and paper.

What makes Angelas style of writing so unique is her realness, anointing, old-age wisdom and personal life experiences. She is completely open about her past, and looks to help other women who may experience similar circumstances as she. She knows there is power in her testimony and she unremorsefully bares it all through her light hearted and thought provoking format.

Fearlessly in pursuit of accomplishing her dreams, Angela is determined more than ever to bring her goals to past! An Ohio State University alumni (OH-IO!), currently receiving her Masters Degree in Science at DePaul University in Chicago, with a focus on digital cinema and film production, Angela is building her empire in 4 inch heels. Recognizing her potential, following Gods lead and fulfilling her purpose, Angela uses her natural talent to inspire women everywhere with her own story. A current resident of Chicago, Illinois by way of Cleveland, Ohio, this single mother of one is the epitome of a woman that's about her business!

For more information, please visit Angelas official website at IamAngelaWilson.com!

To contact Angela for speaking engagements, seminars, book signings, conferences or to send your regards, email Angela at <u>AWilson1569@gmail.com</u>!

Recommended Resources

MISS THANG! IN THE CITY BLOG!

Visit Angelas weekly blog at <u>Missthanginthecity.blogspot.com</u>!

Her blog features everything "fly", from entertainment, lifestyle, inspirational antidotes, Christian biblical teachings, fashion, music, and everything random!

DAUGHTERS OF THE KING, LLC
CHICAGO, ILLINOIS

Angela is launching a new non-profit organization in the city of Chicago, Illinois catered towards minority young girls between the ages of 12-18, but all are welcome! Her foundation focuses on todays issues in young women such as...

* self esteem issues

* relationship with God

* school and college information

* mentoring classes

* and more!

For more information, please contact
DaughtersoftheKingChicago@gmail.com for meeting times,
applications, and events!

Black Diamond Management, LLC.
Euclid, Ohio

A property management company founded by Dionne P. Ashley based just outside Cleveland, Ohio, is a successful up and coming real estate property improvement company. Specializing in the revitalization of deprived urban neighborhoods with an uncanny exquisite talent to maximize the profitability of your properties! Free no obligation consultation!

For more information, please contact: Dionne Ashley at
Dionnepatriceashley@yahoo.com.

Or visit Black Diamonds website at www.Blackdiamond-homes.com!

New Life Covenant Oakwood Church
Chicago, Illinois

Starting in 2004, New Life Covenant Oakwood is one of the fastest growing churches in Chicago! A church based on the Word of God, worship service full of praise and anointing, New Life is a church that provides a "God encounter!" Its community outreach program is one to rival, and senior pastor, John Hannah and beautiful wife Anna, are both a anointed teachers, leaders and living examples.

At Angelas Chicago church home, she knows that once you go New Life, you won't go back!

To find out service times, please visit New Lifes website at www.newlifeoakwood.org.

For more information, please call (773) 285-1731.

Diamond and Pearls Foundation, LLC
Chicago, Illinois

A foundation geared toward the social advancement of young women. It is designed to inspire, educate, and motivate healthy self esteem for teen's girls ages 10 and up. In the past, The Diamond and Pearls Foundation has put on a fund raising fashion show and quarterly meetings, in addition to many fun events!

For more information, please contact Angel English at Sherie1224@gmail.com!

Mt. Sinai Ministries
Cleveland, Ohio

Evangelism, outreach, education, and fellowship all describes this place of God in Cleveland, Ohio. Senior Pastor C.Jay Matthews, first lady and pastor Jacquelyn Matthews are positive instruments to the kingdom of God!

For more information, please visit Mt. Sinai's website at www.mtsinaiministries.org.

Manufactured By: RR Donnelley
                    Breinigsville, PA USA
                    September, 2010